Accession no.
01109066

WARRI

The
Business
Excellence
Handbook

This book is dedicated to the leaders and employees
of The European Foundation for Quality Management,
The American National Institute of Standards and Technology,
The British Quality Foundation,and all those who are
seeking to build better organisations by applying
Business Excellence in the course of their work

The
Business
Excellence
Handbook

Fifth edition

CHESTER COLLEGE
ACC. No. 01109066 DEPT. pbs
CLASS No. 658.4013094 HAK
WARRINGTON LIBRARY
RECEIVED 27 JUL 2004

**Based on the revised
EFQM Excellence Model, 1999**

Chris Hakes

Revised by Steve Bratt and Hugh Gallacher

With contributions from:
Geoff Norris, Mike Parry and Tony Wildman

First edition 1994

Second edition 1995

Third edition 1996

Fourth edition 1997

Fifth edition 1999

© 1994, 1995, 1996, 1997, 1999 BQC Performance Management Ltd (BQC) P.O. Box 175, Ipswich, IP2 8SW,
United Kingdom
Phone: 00 44 (0) 1473 409962
Fax: 00 44 (0) 1473 833303
Email: bqc@bqc-network.com
Website: http://www.bqc-network.com

Published by BQC Performance Management Ltd

ISBN 1 902169 00 X

Apart from any fair dealing for the purposes of research or private study, or criticism or review, as permitted under
the UK Copyright Designs and Patents Act 1988, this publication may not be reproduced, stored, or transmitted,
in any form, or by any means, without the prior permission in writing of BQC, or in the case of reprographic
reproduction only in accordance with the terms of the licences issued by the Copyright Licensing Agency in the UK,
or in accordance with the terms of licences issued by the appropriate Reproduction Rights Organisation outside the UK.
Enquiries concerning reproduction outside the terms stated here should be sent to BQC.

BQC makes no representation, express or implied, with regard to the accuracy of the information contained in this book
and cannot accept any legal responsibility or liability for any errors or omissions that may be made

A catalogue record for this book is available from the British Library.

ema 180500VI.1K

The Business Excellence Handbook

Contents

Acknowledgements

Acknowledgements

The authors involved in this book would like to acknowledge and thank all those who have assisted, influenced, or generally helped to maintain sanity during the production of this book.

Particular thanks are due to our friends and colleagues at EFQM, BQF, NIST, and various regional award schemes. We must also acknowledge the vast range of clients who have helped us in forming these views.

Finally, we thank all those who have assisted in writing, typing, and producing this book. A special thanks goes to Rachel Cook for her dedication above and beyond the call of duty. At times it got the better of us, but luckily not of you.

1   Introduction

Since its introduction at the start of the 1990s, the EFQM Excellence Model has been widely used throughout Europe. From early beginnings in the private sector, its more general applicability across the entire spectrum of organisational life has become clear, and has resulted in its enthusiastic adoption in, for example, the public sector, schools, hospitals, uniformed services, charities, and businesses both large and small.

With the benefit of these experiences, it had become clear that a fundamental review was appropriate, and EFQM completed a wide-ranging review early in 1999. As a result, the Model has been updated and was formally re-launched in April 1999.

This handbook has been fully updated to reflect this improved Model. In addition, we have updated much of the content, and terminology, to reflect current practice. Thus, the title of this volume has been changed from 'The Corporate Self Assessment Handbook' to 'The Business Excellence Handbook' to avoid confusion with the term 'self-assessment' as now used by the UK tax authorities. Its sister volume 'Organisational Self Assessment for Public Sector Excellence' has become 'The Public Sector Excellence Handbook'.

We believe the improved Model will rapidly win favour for several reasons: -

First, the improved Model has a number of features that will increase its appeal non-profit making organisations, particularly in its use of 'organisational' rather than 'business' language.

Second, we believe that the emphasis on partnerships will broaden its appeal in an environment where both commercial and non-commercial organisations increasingly rely on long-term two-way relationships to achieve their mutual objectives.

Third, the emphasis on knowledge and innovation will appeal to the increasing number of organisations who grow and prosper as a result of exploiting information and leading edge technology.

Fourth, the new scoring mechanism, the so-called RADAR card, makes a stronger case for the existence of closed-loop improvement cycles.

Overall, we believe the revised Model brings new challenges for existing users, and brings features that will increase its appeal in sectors where interest has, to date, been relatively limited. We hope that this Handbook will therefore be equally helpful to both existing practitioners of Business Excellence, and to those approaching it for the first time.

The structure of the Handbook

This edition of the Handbook has also been fundamentally reviewed, and has been restructured in response to feedback we have received on previous editions. The structure we have adopted follows a hypothetical implementation path for an organisation choosing to adopt Business Excellence: -

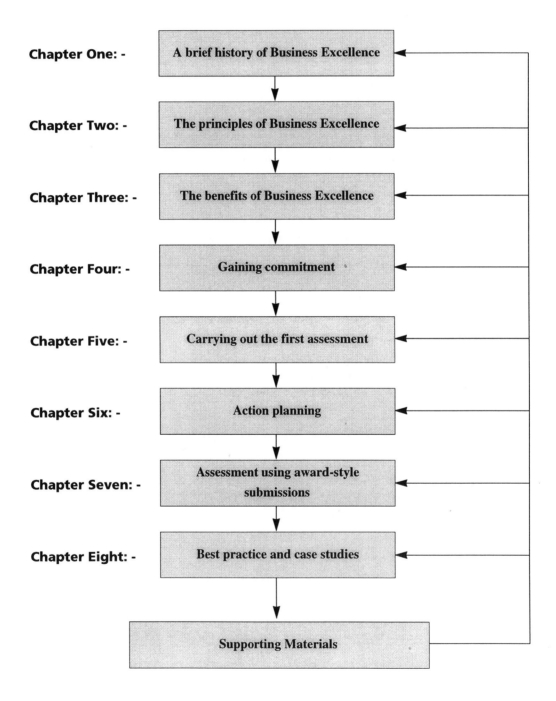

Chapter One begins with a brief history of Business Excellence, which is primarily aimed at readers who are new to the subject. This section is intended to provide sufficient background to enable readers to put Business Excellence into an appropriate context with other business improvement methodologies.

In Chapter Two, we examine some of the underlying principles of Business Excellence, and then describe how these have been reflected in the improved Model.

This is followed in Chapter Three by a description of the benefits that previous users have found from using Business Excellence.

Then, in Chapter Four, we examine approaches to gaining commitment to Business Excellence. This covers issues such as raising awareness, and dealing with any barriers.

In Chapter Five, we review the various approaches to carrying out the first assessment within an organisation, ranging from simple questionnaire-based assessments, to more sophisticated workshop-based events.

In Chapter Six, we consider how to translate the organisation's first assessment into an action plan, and suggest how this might be implemented and integrated into the business.

Chapter Seven first covers the use of award-style reports to conduct internal assessments. While many organisations are deterred from this approach by the apparent amount of effort needed to create a 75-page document as required by the European and UK Awards, several regional Awards are working with shorter report formats. It then goes on to consider applying for an award, and look in brief at managing a site visit.

Chapter Eight looks at best practice. We include reports on how various organisations have approached Business Excellence. In addition, we have included, for the first time, extracts from BQC's database of best practice.

Finally, the Handbook ends with appendices which contain detailed material on using the improved Model, and a resource kit to lead the reader through all the steps necessary to gather data for an assessment.

The approach taken in this book is deliberately practical, and is informed by BQC's experience with many clients over the years. These include several European and UK Award winners, and a very broad range of organisations in the Public Sector.

Links to other BQC publications

BQC has published a number of detailed guides to aspects of Business Excellence, since the last edition of this Handbook. Some information from these guides has been incorporated in this book. In particular, the description of the various types of assessment workshops in Chapter Five is partly based on material from 'The Facilitator Support Kit'. The creation of award-style documents described in Chapter Seven borrows from 'The Submission Writer's Handbook'. The section on best practice data in Chapter Eight is extracted from much more detailed data in 'The Excellence Routefinder'.

Details of these, and other BQC publications are to be found in the final Appendix.

Chapter One:

A Brief History of Business Excellence

Origins in Japan

The origins of Business Excellence date back almost fifty years, and can be traced back over three continents. The growth of Japan as a major economic force in the last quarter of this century has been partly ascribed to the way in which its manufacturing industry has systematically adopted Company-Wide Quality Control techniques. Application of this disciplined approach to managing consistency and quality in Japan was the test bed for the ideas of perhaps the most famous quality gurus, W. Edwards Deming and Joseph Juran. As this work began to show benefit in the early 1950s, the Japanese Union of Scientists and Engineers (JUSE) instituted the Deming Prize to recognise both organisations and individuals who had made an exemplary contribution to excellence using statistical quality control techniques. For many years, these awards were restricted to Japanese nationals, but in 1984, a prize has been available to recognise non-Japanese organisations. The first such winner was Florida Power and Light in 1989, followed by Phillips Taiwan in 1992, and AT&T in 1994. While this is undoubtedly the first recognisable 'Business Excellence Model', its use as an internal process within organisations has been limited as the assessment process is generally poorly understood outside Japan.

Interest grows in the West

The Deming Prize approach stood alone for many years, until Japan had made major inroads into many Western economies. The need to compete became clear in the West, and in 1983 a White House Conference on Productivity was held, with keynote speeches from President Reagan, Vice President Bush and Commerce Secretary Malcolm Baldrige. The report published following the conference opened with a very blunt headline statement:

> *'America is the most productive nation in the world, but its growth in productivity has faltered. Some of the factors contributing to slower productivity growth are within our control and some are not, but it is important that we respond to this challenge.'*

A long and wide-ranging debate ensued, and resulted in agreement from both political and business leaders that corporate excellence should be recognised through the establishment of a highly prestigious national award presented annually by the President. Thus, the Malcolm Baldrige National Quality Award (MBNQA) was launched in 1988. The criteria for the award framework were developed by taking the best from other business standards and models, including the Deming Prize, and through lengthy consultation with leaders in the business community. The criteria established by this approach thus reflected a consensus of what best practice looked like at the time, and an annual review process was put in place to ensure that the Baldrige Model continues to reflect evolving trends.

Although the award was perhaps the more visible outcome of the Baldrige Model, in practice, the vast majority of users of the Model do so within their organisations, with no intent to apply for an award. Indeed, the number of applications for the award has only once exceeded one hundred in the eleven years it has existed.

Part of the success and popularity of the Model is due to the development of case studies of excellence, based on real-life examples. In addition, assessor training is widely available, and serves to develop and calibrate teams of assessors, who can apply this learning both to their own organisations and to award applicants. One particularly powerful aspect of the approach is its reliance on teams of assessors to reach a consensus view of the assessed organisation's strengths, areas for improvement, and scores against the Model. This assessment, based on an award application document, is used to decide which of the applicants will receive a site visit, and ultimately provides a basis for selecting the award winners.

The Malcolm Baldrige National Quality Award was first presented in 1988. Two awards are available in each of the three categories of Manufacturing, Service and Small Organisations. The winners to date are shown in Diagram 1.1.

Diagram 1.1: Malcolm Baldrige Award winners

1988: -

Manufacturing: -	Motorola Inc. Westinghouse Commercial Nuclear Fuels Division
Service: -	No Award
Small organisations: -	Globe Metallurgical

1989: -

Manufacturing: -	Milliken and Company Xerox Corporation
Service: -	No Award
Small organisations: -	No Award

1990: -

Manufacturing: -	Cadillac Motor Car Company IBM Rochester
Service: -	Federal Express Corporation
Small organisations: -	Wallace Co. Inc.

1991: -

Manufacturing: -	Solectron Corporation Zytec Corporation
Service: -	No Award
Small organisations: -	Marlow Industries

1992: -	Manufacturing: -	AT&T Network Systems Group, Transmission Systems Business Unit Texas Instruments Inc., Defense systems and Electronics Group
	Service: -	AT&T Universal Card Services The Ritz-Carlton Hotel Company
	Small organisations: -	Granite Rock Company
1993: -	Manufacturing: -	Eastman Chemical Company
	Service: -	No Award
	Small organisations: -	Ames Rubber Corporation
1994: -	Manufacturing: -	No Award
	Service: -	AT&T Consumer Communications Services GTE Directories Corporation
	Small organisations: -	Wainwright Industries Inc.
1995: -	Manufacturing: -	Armstrong World Industries, Building Products Division Corning Telecommunications Products Division
	Service: -	No Award
	Small organisations: -	No Award
1996: -	Manufacturing: -	ADAC Laboratories
	Service: -	Dana Commercial Credit Corporation
	Small organisations: -	Customer Research Inc. Trident Precision Manufacturing Inc.
1997: -	Manufacturing: -	3M Dental Products Solectron Corporation
	Service: -	Merrill Lynch Credit Xerox Business Services
	Small organisations: -	No Award
1998: -	Manufacturing: -	Boeing Airlift and Tanker Programs Solar Turbines
	Service: -	No Award
	Small organisations: -	Texas Nameplate

Over the years, The Baldrige Model has evolved to reflect changing expectations. From a start where it was firmly rooted in quality, its focus shifted some time ago to performance excellence, based on a process-oriented approach to quality management. In the last year or so, the focus has shifted again to the overall quality of management.

From the start, there have been questions about whether using the Baldrige Model actually 'works'. Is it possible to demonstrate that use of the Model leads to success in business?

In practice, it is thought unlikely that a methodology can be devised to provide objective proof. But, for some years, the US Commerce Department's National Institute of Standards and Technology has constructed a fictitious stock fund, made up of all those publicly-traded companies who have won the award.

In 1998, and for the fifth successive year, this fictitious portfolio outperformed the Standard and Poor's 500 Index by 260%, achieving a 426% return on investment, compared with a 173% return for the Index as a whole. Is this consistent outperformance of the Index a causal and conclusive proof? Maybe not, but it is at very least a powerful indication that application of a holistic approach to Business Excellence CAN result in high levels of business performance!

Developments in Europe

Development of a European approach followed quickly on from the Baldrige experience. In September 1988, the leaders of fourteen major European companies played a major role in establishing the European Foundation for Quality Management (EFQM). About a year later, EFQM was officially launched, with an objective to promote Total Quality and Business Excellence throughout Europe, and to support its members in their efforts to achieve excellence. EFQM established its own Model, learning from the Deming and Baldrige approaches. Perhaps its most significant innovation was to introduce a requirement to demonstrate improved business results. The Model (Diagram 1.2) was based on the principle that: -

> *'Customer satisfaction, people satisfaction, and impact on society are achieved through leadership driving policy and strategy, people management, resources and processes, leading ultimately to excellence in business results'*

In addition, and learning from the Baldrige process, it was made clear from the start that the prime purpose of the Model was to help organisations to improve. Running an award process is clearly a part of that purpose, by identifying aspirational role models, and pushing back the boundaries of best practice each year.

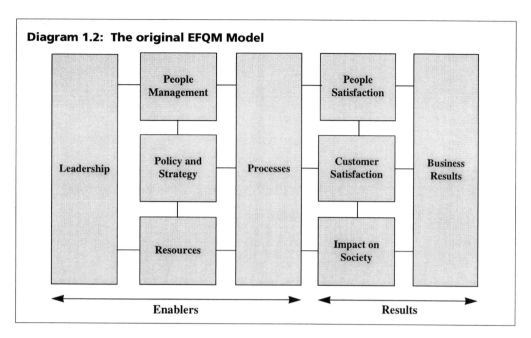

Diagram 1.2: The original EFQM Model

Leadership	People Management	Processes	People Satisfaction	Business Results
	Policy and Strategy		Customer Satisfaction	
	Resources		Impact on Society	

← Enablers → ← Results →

In 1991, EFQM launched The European Quality Award as a prestigious competition, open to all commercial organisations in Europe. To win the award, applicants must satisfy an independent jury that they can outperform all others in meeting the requirements of the Model, and demonstrate that they have contributed significantly to satisfying the expectations of their customers, employees, and other stakeholders who have an interest in the organisation. Each year several prizes are awarded. The Award itself is presented to the organisation judged to be the best of the prize winners - the most successful exponent of Business Excellence in Europe.

Diagram1.3 shows the award and prize winners to date.

Diagram. 1.3: European Award and prize winners

Year	Award Winner	Prize winners
1992	Rank Xerox	BOC-Special gases UBISA
1993	Milliken European Division	ICL Manufacturing Division
1994	Design to Distribution Ltd	Ericsson SA IBM SEMEA
1995	Texas Instruments (Europe)	TNT Express (UK) Ltd
1996	Brisa	BT Netas TNT Express (UK)
1997	SGS - Thomson BEKSA (SME)	BT Netas TNT (UK) Gasnalsa (SME)
1998	TNT (UK) Landhotel Schindlerhof (SME) Beko Trading Co. (SME)	BT Northern Ireland Netas Sollac BT Yellow Pages AVE (Public Sector) Inland Revenue Accounts Office, Cumbernauld (Public Sector) Di EU (SME)

The UK perspective

In 1992, The UK Secretary of State for Trade and Industry established a committee chaired by Sir Denys Henderson (then Chairman of ICI plc) to

'consider and report...on the feasibility of developing a new prestigous award for British business, building on the existing British Quality Award, and, if the feasibility is confirmed, to make recommendations for the subsequent introduction and development of the award.'

The Henderson Committee reviewed the various approaches available at that time, and proposed that the European framework should be adopted. As a result, the British Quality Foundation (BQF) was established in November 1992. Its aim is to enhance the performance and effectiveness of organisations in the UK through the promotion of proven quality techniques that improve business results.

In 1994, BQF introduced the UK Quality Award (UKQA) as a means of identifying, rewarding and publicising outstanding organisations that are role models for Business Excellence. The Award scheme, and the underlying Business Excellence Model, provide a framework for all organisations, regardless of sector, to assess themselves, to identify areas for improvement, and ultimately, to achieve the level of the best.

The Award is run annually and a small number of equal status awards are made. The UK award now comprises a range of awards to reflect large companies, Public sector organisations, small and medium sized organisations, (50-250 staff) and those with less than 50 staff. Diagram 1.4 shows the winning organisations to date.

Diagram.1.4: UK award winners

Year	Award Winner	Sector
1994	Rover	Private,>250 employees
	TNT Express (UK) Ltd	Private,>250 employees
1995	ICL High Performance Technology	Private,>250 employees
1996	Mortgage Express	Private,>250 employees
	Ulster Carpet Mills	Private,>250 employees
1997	BT Business Division	Private,>250 employees
	BT Northern Ireland	Private,>250 employees
	Hewlett Packard	Private,>250 employees
	The Dell Primary School	Public,<250 employees
1998	BT Payphones	Private,>250 employees
	Nortel (Northern Ireland)	Private,>250 employees
	The Seaview Hotel & Restaurant Isle of Wight	Private,<50 employees

Throughout Europe, national bodies similar to the British Quality Foundation have been formed, and have adopted the Business Excellence Model as their framework.

Diagram. 1.5: European countries using the Business Excellence Model			
Austria	Germany	Norway	Slovenia
Belgium	Hungary	The Netherlands	Spain
Croatia	Iceland	Portugal	Switzerland
Czech Republic	Ireland	Russia	Turkey
Denmark	Italy	Slovak Republic	Ukraine
			United Kingdom

Three countries have adopted different Models, incorporating some Baldrige criteria. These are France, Finland, and Sweden. It should be noted that the differences between the Baldrige and EFQM Models are becoming smaller and smaller, as the two organisations work together, and observers consider that the two Models differ in only about 5% of their overall content.

In addition, within the UK, a range of regional bodies have developed local award schemes based on the Business Excellence Model.

Diagram.1.6: Regional Awards in the UK		
Scotland	North East	South West
Northern Ireland	Midlands	East of England
Wales	Meridian	London
North West	Yorkshire	

Thus, in less than ten years, the principles of Business Excellence have permeated organisational life from one end of Europe to the other, and from the largest global enterprises, major parts of government, public sector agencies, healthcare, schools, police authorities, to the research laboratory, the professions, and the small business. To have this appeal, the underlying principles of the Model must reflect widely-held views on best organisational practice. It is to those underlying principles, and how they have been reflected in the improved Model, that we turn in the next chapter.

Chapter Two:

The principles of Business Excellence and the improved Model

Introduction

Given the extent to which Business Excellence has been adopted, its underlying principles and values must be widely perceived as beneficial and relevant to organisations today. That, in itself, is testimony to its enduring value, as the organisational climate today has moved on dramatically since the Model was first introduced.

Few would disagree that the competitive challenge facing organisations today has little precedent. Technology has driven the development of products limited only by our imagination, and flexible manufacturing techniques can customise that product to an individual's specification. Time-to-market has become a key differentiator of success, and products, for example software, can be developed round the clock, starting in the Far East, moving on to Europe, and then to the West Coast of the USA as the day passes. Improvements in logistics can deliver that product overnight, from halfway across the globe. Developments in communications and information technology can provide near instantaneous service, at any hour of the day or night. As customers experience one example of world-class performance, or service, their expectations inexorably rise to expect the same in all their transactions.

Shareholders, too, have come to expect a high level of returns from their investment, based on the performance of most of the world's stockmarkets over the last thirty years or more. This has driven organisations in many business sectors to realise that shareholder expectations are unlikely to be satisfied by organic growth, and has led to an unprecedented level of mergers and acquisitions. We see little sign of this trend abating in the future.

People's expectations of the world of work continue to increase with increasing affluence. We are no longer satisfied with a steady, secure income. Those with jobs are spending longer and longer at work, and the boundaries between work and home are increasingly blurred. One consequence is that people are expecting to achieve more meaning, satisfaction and personal growth from their working lives. Several sectors of business already find it challenging to employ the people they need on terms that people are prepared to accept. We ignore these increasing expectations at our peril.

And finally, society has increasing expectations of organisations. We not only expect them to neutralise any adverse impact they may have on our environment, but also to recognise and contribute to the development of a society that we cannot sustain as individuals. As the prime creators of wealth, organisations are increasingly the target as we strive to create a fairer society. To their credit, many organisations have recognised that they do not exist in isolation from society, and are playing an increasingly active role.

Survival and growth (and therefore a sustained future) thus depend on balancing these demanding, and sometimes competing, needs in a very responsive way. It is a complex equation, shifting on a daily basis, and demanding flexibility, efficiency, consistency, effectiveness, innovation, and agility. These, and a host of other virtues, are the constituent features of success that underpin Business Excellence.

In reviewing and revising the Model the EFQM have ensured that it aligns with their 8 Fundamental Concepts of Performance Excellence. The following is a brief overview of these concepts which are encapsulated in the Model.

Customer focus

Customer focus is a strategic concept. It is directed towards customer retention and gains in market share. It demands constant sensitivity to emerging customer and market requirements, and measurement of the factors that drive customer satisfaction, loyalty and retention. It also demands awareness of developments in technology, and rapid and flexible responses to customer and market requirements.

"The Award and self assessment is a means to the crucial end of helping UK companies develop a competitive edge by satisfying the needs of customers, shareholders, employees and the community, in which they operate"

-Sir Denys Henderson Former Chairman ICI and Zeneca

Meeting or exceeding customer expectations not only deliver a one-off sale but also build a perceived quality image in the market place. Analysis of the 'Profit Impact of Market Strategies Database' (financial and strategic information on 3,000 businesses world-wide), has shown that perceived service quality is an important factor in business success. Results show that the market leaders charge an average of almost ten per cent more for their products and services, increase their businesses twice as fast, and boost market share by an average of six per cent per year. Additionally, customers are five times more likely to switch vendors because of perceived service problems rather than as a result of price concerns or product quality issues. And since it costs five times as much to gain a new customer as it does to keep an existing one, it makes good financial sense to improve your processes and to take care of customers when they encounter problems.

Continuous learning, improvement and innovation

Achieving the highest levels of quality and competitiveness requires a well-defined and well-executed approach to continuous review and improvement of all aspects of the company's operation. The term continuous improvement refers to both ongoing, incremental and major, breakthrough improvements. A focus on improvement and relevant knowledge management practices needs to be part of all operations and of all work units within a company. For many organisations the concept of continuous improvement can be epitomised by the Plan/Do/Check/Act concept as applied to discrete problems, processes, or the company as a whole.

"We'll have to learn from the mistakes that others make. We can't live long enough to make them all ourselves

-Anon

Any approach to improvement and learning needs to be 'embedded' in the way the company functions. Embedded means that improvement:

- is part of the daily work of all units;
- processes seek to eliminate problems at their source;
- is driven by opportunities to do better, as well as by problems that must be corrected.

Improvement should be driven not only by the objective to provide better product and service quality, but also by the need to be responsive and efficient - both conferring vital market place advantages.

An organisation needs to be outward looking, learn from others and manage its knowledge base to ensure it is genuinely innovative.

People development and involvement

An organisation's success in meeting its quality and performance objectives depends increasingly on the level and standard of involvement of the whole work force. For this reason, employee satisfaction measurement provides an important indicator of the success of a company's improvement efforts. Improving performance requires employee development at all levels.

Organisations need to invest in the development of the work force and to seek new avenues to involve employees in improvement activities and decision making. Factors that bear upon the safety, health, well being and morale of employees need to be part of the organisation's continuous improvement objectives. Increasingly, training and participation need to be tailored to a more diverse work force, and to more flexible work structures that encourage empowerment of all employees.

Organisations can invest significantly in systems, technology, re-engineered processes and the like, but without the commitment, empowerment and involvement of their people, they will not reach their full potential.

Management by processes and facts

The basic or operational processes that create an organisation's products or services determine the quality of those products or services. If the chain of processes is made efficient and effective, and adds value, then the resulting products or services will also be efficient and effective.

A process management approach is designed to enable managers to optimise the inter-relationships of functional organisations and to focus on the value-added factors of all process elements. In addition, it promotes the development of a 'preventative culture' by emphasising that continuous improvement and corrective action (action to eliminate the cause of an existing or potential problem and to prevent its re-occurrence) are goals at early stages in all activities.

Typically, efforts become directed primarily towards controlling the processes, rather than towards direct, specific controls of products, services, or, even worse, people. Applying direct product and service controls, such as inspection, often addresses only symptoms of potential problems, neglecting causes that lie within the process itself.

Concentrating on process management creates more efficient processes and lower costs. More effective processes produce higher quality services, gain more satisfied customers and increase market share.

Achievement of world class performance goals requires the use of reliable information and analysis to support, review and change beliefs, opinions, convictions and decisions. Facts needed for improvement and assessment can be gleaned from many aspects of a company's activity including:

- customers and customer feedback;
- product and service performance;
- operations;
- market and economic environment;
- comparisons with competitors and/or companies which exhibit a 'best in class' approach to the process or activity under review;
- suppliers;
- employees;
- financial sources and resources.

> *"A wise man recognises the convenience of a general statement, but he bows to the authority of a particular fact"*
>
> *-Oliver Wendell Holmes 1872*

Analysis may entail using data to reveal information - such as trends, projections, and cause and effect - that might not otherwise be evident. Facts and analysis should support a variety of organisational activities, such as planning, reviewing performance, improving operations, and comparing performance with that of competitors or with best practice benchmarks.

Results orientation

A major element in improving performance involves the creation and use of performance indicators. These are measurable characteristics of products, services, processes and operations, used by an organisation to evaluate and improve performance and to track progress. The measures and results used ought to be guided and balanced by the interests of all stakeholders - customers, employees, stockholders, suppliers and partners, the public, and the community. The use of a balanced combination of performance indicators offers an effective means to communicate requirements, to monitor actual performance, and to marshal support for improving results.

Leadership and constancy of purpose

An organisation's leaders must create customer oriented, clear and visible organisation values and high expectations. Reinforcement of these values and expectations requires substantial personal commitment and involvement. Leaders must take part in the creation of corporate strategies, plans and systems for achieving excellence. Through regular personal involvement in visible activities, such as planning, communications, reviews of corporate excellence performance, and recognising employees for their achievement, leaders serve as role models reinforcing the values and encouraging leadership in all levels of employee.

> *"Managers manage within a paradigm. Leaders lead between paradigms"*
>
> *-Anon*

Mutually beneficial partnerships

Organisations should seek to build external partnerships to accomplish their overall goals. Examples of partnerships could include those with competitors, customers, suppliers and educational organisations. For success partnerships need to be based on trust, knowledge sharing and an integrated approach.

Partnerships should seek to develop longer-term objectives, and create a basis for mutual investment and growth. Partners should address the key requirements for success of the partnership, methods of regular communication, approaches to evaluating progress, and the means for adapting to changing conditions.

Public responsibility

This concept relates to basic expectations the community has of the organisations that serve it. Within organisations, plans should exist to seek avenues to avoid problems, to measure the perception that the community at large has of the organisation, to provide a forthright organisation response if problems occur, and to make available information needed to maintain public awareness, safety, trust, and confidence.

Corporate citizenship requires the organisation to take a leading role - within the reasonable limits of its resources - to address activities including education, resource conservation, support of community services, and the improvement of industrial and business practices. Excellent organisations go beyond the minimum regulatory requirements for the sector in which they operate.

An effective organisation should monitor the results, and number, of its approaches to public responsibility and the ultimate perception society has of its impact on society.

The pressure for change

The Model clearly needs to reflect changing views of excellence, and, indeed, is reviewed annually. A decision was made in 1996 to conduct a more fundamental review. In the next section, we examine the development process, and consider the detailed changes in the improved Model.

Development of the Improved Model

Background

At the topmost level, the overall theme and language of the Model has evolved. Continuing a trend started some years ago, and mirrored in the Baldrige Model, references to 'Total Quality' are now almost absent, and the term 'Business Excellence' is becoming 'Organisational Excellence'. EFQM define 'Organisational Excellence' as

> *'The overall way of working that results in balanced stakeholder (customers, employees, partners, society, shareholders) satisfaction, so increasing the probability of long term success as an organisation'*

The need for a more outwardly focused, holistic approach has grown consistently in recent years, and it became clear that the Business Excellence Model should undergo a more rigorous and fundamental review than was customarily carried out each year. Thus, a process to develop an improved Model was set in place in early 1997.

The process

Development of the improved Model started in January 1997. A fifteen-member committee, from nine member states, was created, and met for the first of what was to become twenty meetings in July 1997.

As input to the development process, they had results from, or commissioned, member surveys in 1996, 1997 and 1998. These gathered responses from over 500 organisations and individuals. In addition, over 1000 organisations and individuals offered additional comments during 1997 and 1998, gathered by a variety of workshops, round table discussions, and from award assessor feedback.

This gave the committee about 10,000 ideas for improving the Model. These were grouped into thirteen clusters, using a concept mapping approach, and this ultimately resulted in about 100 key statements.

Analysis of these statements resulted in a decision to maintain the existing nine-criterion Model, and to retain the concept of criterion parts. The content of several of these was, however, substantially changed.

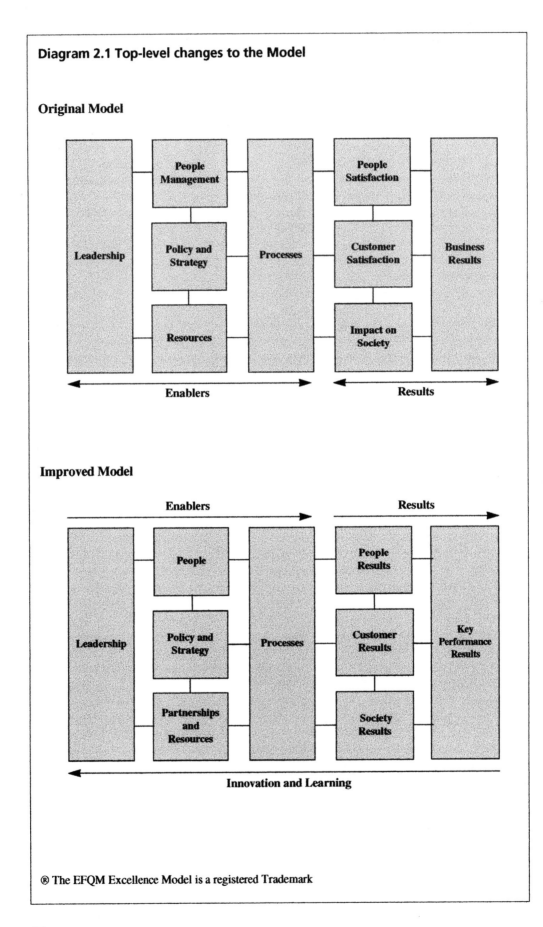

Diagram 2.1 Top-level changes to the Model

Original Model

	Enablers			Results	
Leadership	People Management / Policy and Strategy / Resources	Processes	People Satisfaction / Customer Satisfaction / Impact on Society	Business Results

Improved Model

	Enablers			Results	
Leadership	People / Policy and Strategy / Partnerships and Resources	Processes	People Results / Customer Results / Society Results	Key Performance Results

Innovation and Learning

® The EFQM Excellence Model is a registered Trademark

In the rest of this Chapter, we examine the changes at an individual sub-criterion level, and draw some conclusions about the impact these changes may have.

Diagram 2.2.

LEADERSHIP	
Existing Model	*Improved Model*
1a. How leaders visibly demonstrate their commitment to excellence and continuous improvement.	1a. Leaders develop the mission, vision and values and are role models of a culture of Excellence.
1b. How leaders support improvement and involvement by providing appropriate resources and assistance.	1b. Leaders are personally involved in ensuring the organisation's management system is developed, implemented and continuously improved.
1c. How leaders are involved with their customers, suppliers and other external organisations.	1c. Leaders are involved with customers, partners and representatives of society.
1d. How leaders recognise and appreciate people's efforts and achievements.	1d. Leaders motivate, support and recognise the organisation's people.

Two important additions are made to this criterion.

First, it is clearly the responsibility of leaders to give purpose and direction to the organisation, and evidence of how this is done is now required in sub-criterion 1a. This is looking to see how strategic direction is set.

Second, it is a leadership responsibility to define, develop and implement the organisation's overall management system. Sub-criterion 1b looks to leaders to develop and implement the processes which will enable them to deliver the overall strategy.

Diagram 2.3.

POLICY AND STRATEGY	
Existing Model	*Improved Model*
2a. How policy and strategy are based on information which is relevant and comprehensive.	2a. Policy and Strategy are based on the present and future needs and expectations of stakeholders.
2b. How policy and strategy are developed.	2b. Policy and Strategy are based on information from performance measurement, research, learning and creativity-related activities.
2c. How policy and strategy are communicated and implemented.	2c. Policy and Strategy are developed, reviewed and updated.
2d. How policy and strategy are regularly updated and improved.	2d. Policy and Strategy are deployed through a framework of key processes.
	2e. Policy and Strategy are communicated and implemented.

This criterion has been further clarified. The requirement for policy and strategy to be based on relevant information has been split into (1) stakeholder information and (2) information from internal performance, knowledge and learning.

Stakeholder information is predominantly focused on the customer, but also, of course, includes shareholders, partners, employees, and society. This emphasis is consistent with a general theme, throughout the improved Model, of increased customer focus.

The emphasis on performance measurements, knowledge and learning, highlights the need to demonstrate that policy and strategy are based on disciplined analysis of the data.

The need to show how policy and strategy are deployed through key processes consolidates an approach that was previously spread across criteria two and five.

Diagram 2.4.

PEOPLE	
Existing Model	**Improved Model**
3a. How people resources are planned and improved.	3a. People resources are planned, managed and improved.
3b. How people capabilities are sustained and developed.	3b. People's knowledge and competencies are identified, developed and sustained.
3c. How people agree targets and continuously review performance.	3c. People are involved and empowered.
3d. How people are involved, empowered and recognised.	3d. People and the organisation have a dialogue.
3e. How people and the organisation have an effective dialogue.	3e. People are rewarded, recognised and cared for.
3f. How people are cared for.	

In this area, sub-criterion 3a has been expanded. In addition to the previous requirement to show how people resources are planned and improved, the improved Model requires evidence of how people resources are managed at the topmost level.

In addition, there is an increased focus in sub-criterion 3b on showing how knowledge is managed and how competence is developed. The original sub-criterion addressing target setting has now been integrated into sub-criterion 3b.

Sub-criterion 3e now emphasises that cultural development is not based solely on recognition processes, but is also supported by the reward systems.

Diagram 2.5.

PARTNERSHIPS & RESOURCES	
Existing Model	*Improved Model*
4a. How financial resources are managed.	4a. External partnerships are managed.
4b. How information resources are managed.	4b. Finances are managed.
4c. How supplier relationships and materials are managed.	4c. Buildings, equipment and materials are managed.
4d. How buildings, equipment and other assets are managed.	4d. Technology is managed.
4e. How technology is managed.	4e. Information and knowledge are managed.

The key addition to this criterion is the recognition that partnerships play an increasingly important part of life in many organisations. Partnerships are focused on key suppliers and other organisations with whom joint working is important for success.

Examples might include outsourcing of IT support, strategic alliances with owners of specialised proprietary technology, as is particularly evident at present in pharmaceutical R + D. Many logistics 'total solutions' relating to JIT delivery and the consolidation of assembly kits in high technology manufacturing, as is the case in several aerospace-related industries.

Again, as elsewhere in the improved Model, the emphasis in the 'information resources' sub-criterion now includes knowledge, as well as information.

Diagram 2.6.

PROCESSES	
Existing Model	*Improved Model*
5a. How processes key to the success of the organisation are identified.	5a. Processes are systematically designed and managed.
5b. How processes are systematically managed.	5b. Processes are improved, as needed, using innovation in order to fully satisfy and generate increasing value for customers and other stakeholders.
5c. How the processes are reviewed and targets set for improvement.	
5d. How processes are improved using innovation and creativity.	5c. Products and Services are designed and developed based on customer needs and expectations.
5e. How processes are changed and the benefits evaluated.	5d. Products and Services are produced, delivered and serviced.
	5e. Customer relationships are managed and enhanced..

The revision of this criterion, coupled with that of criterion two, are two of the major developments in the improved Model.

The Model now looks for evidence that processes are systematically designed, as well as managed, in order to translate the organisation's policy and strategy into action.

There is an increased emphasis (in sub-criteria 5c, 5d and 5e) on those processes that have a direct impact on the needs of the customer. The Model now highlights the design and development of products and services, their production, delivery, and ongoing servicing, and management of the overall customer relationship.

Diagram 2.7.

CUSTOMER RESULTS	
Existing Model	*Improved Model*
6a. The customers' perception of the organisationís products, services and customer relationships.	6a. Perception Measures.
6b. Additional measures relating to the satisfaction of the organisationís customers.	6b. Performance Indicators.

There are no major changes to this criterion.

Diagram 2.8.

PEOPLE RESULTS	
Existing Model	*Improved Model*
7a. The people's perception of the organisation.	7a. Perception Measures.
7b. Additional measures relating to people satisfaction.	7b. Performance Indicators

There are no major changes to this criterion, although sub-criterion 7b now includes a focus on employee achievements as a performance indicator.

Diagram 2.9.

SOCIETY RESULTS	
Existing Model	*Improved Model*
8a. Society's perception of the organisation.	8a. Perception Measures.
8b. Additional indicators of the organisation's impact on society	8b. Performance Indicators

There are no major changes to this criterion. Note that 'accolades and awards' have been moved from sub-criterion 8a to 8b.

Diagram 2.10.

KEY PERFORMANCE RESULTS	
Existing Model	*Improved Model*
9a. Financial measures of the organisation's performance. 9b. Additional measures of the organisation's performance.	9a. Key Performance Outcomes. 9b. Key Performance Indicators

This is the only 'results' criterion to be significantly changed.

Previously this criterion was separated into financial and non-financial business results.

Now sub-criterion 9a covers 'key performance outcomes', the key results planned by the organisation's objectives and goals, as defined by its policy and strategy. Another way to view outcomes is to see them as the 'end results'.

Sub-criterion 9b now covers 'key performance indicators'; those results that can be considered as predictors of the key performance outcomes. These are the key process measures used to drive towards the end results.

Note that 9a and 9b now both include financial and non-financial measures.

Summary

These changes to the Model became available to members during April 1999, although the 1999 award processes will continue to use the original Model until the 2000 cycle of awards. In the remainder of this book, we will work with the Improved Model throughout, although historical material, (for example, case studies), reflect the original Model.

Chapter Three:

The benefits of using Business Excellence

Introduction

The Business Excellence Model does not prescribe a course of action, but instead offers a proven framework based on principles that appear to be relevant to a wide range of organisations. As we have also seen, development of the Improved Model has also given an opportunity to augment these principles to reflect the current 'state of the art'.

Thus it is an approach continually informed by best practice and new developments. It is likely to be the most up-to-date guide available to the executive manager. But what benefits does it bring?

For some time, our view has been that the benefits of Business Excellence are based more on management perception than objective proof. Therefore, in 1993, we began research into the benefits that leading practitioners claimed to have obtained from applying the Model. This was almost entirely based on private sector results. Since this initial study, we have gathered further data as use of the Model has spread widely into the public sector and non-profit making organisations.

The benefits claimed by leading practitioners have remained remarkably stable over the years. In descending order these are: -

---

Diagram 3.1: The benefits of using Business Excellence

1. To measure holistic performance and target future improvements
2. To identify and share best practice
3. To create a vision of excellence and common language to achieve it
4. To respond more effectively to customer requirements
5. To gain public recognition by winning awards
6. To make inter-site and inter-divisional comparisons

It is interesting to note that the strongest benefit is focused on using the Model internally within the organisation, while gaining public recognition by winning awards is well down the list. While the trend in applications for the various awards is upwards in 1999, and shows particularly strong growth in some of the newer regional awards, it is clear that most users value internal improvement much more strongly than a moment of glory. This picture is equally clear in the USA, where applications for the Malcolm Baldrige award grew to a peak of 106 in 1991, and have since gradually declined to 36 in 1998.

We now examine each of the benefits above in more detail: -

To measure holistic performance and target future improvements

An assessment against the Business Excellence Model provides a detailed and specific set of strengths and areas for improvement, and a score that is objectively calibrated against best practice.

There can be no improvement where there are no standards. The starting point in any improvement is to know exactly where one stands"

Masaaki Imai

These results can be used by organisations to prioritise and target improvements, and measure their progress towards excellence. More experienced practitioners have integrated the improvement initiatives identified by the assessment into the organisation's strategies and plans, and use the Business Excellence Model as a framework for their strategic management process, for example by appointing 'criterion owners' at a strategic level. This ensures a continued focus on the criteria of the Model, and an ongoing 'balance' in the organisation's activities. Integration in this way naturally leads to a cycle of improvement and regular assessment against the Model, linked to the organisation's business planning cycle.

These organisations recognise that the benefit of the Model is to provide a framework that is stretching yet non-prescriptive. For many organisations, the score achieved in an initial assessment is sufficient motivation to realise that the pace of improvement must be accelerated. On several occasions, practitioners have noted that the pace of improvement in their organisations at least doubled when they adopted Business Excellence. For others, the recognition that they perform creditably in some criterion parts of the Model is sufficient to focus them on areas where the need for improvement is more urgent.

To identify and share best practice

To score well in the 'results' criteria in the Model, organisations must show that they compare their performance with others, and indeed, that their performance is superior. This drives most users to establish a systematic benchmarking process. By making comparisons externally (and, for that matter, internally) organisations can identify where they can learn from the practices of others. Much has been written about the various approaches to benchmarking. In many cases, comparison of the underlying processes being benchmarked is often the most fertile source of improvement ideas.

"Everyone takes the limits of his or her own field of vision for the limits of the world"

-Arthur Schopenauer philosopher

In addition, the common language of the Business Excellence Model has brought an opportunity to compare approaches at the criterion part level. Thus, for example, a computer company can see how a chemical company has addressed the management of waste materials in criterion part 4c. These comparisons have been aided by the publication of award applications by many award winners.

Understandably, these are often edited versions, with financially- or strategically-sensitive information removed, but these nevertheless provide a deep insight into best practice, and are also of great value when considering the compilation of an award-style document for either internal or external assessment (Diagram 3.2).

Diagram 3.2: Published Award-winning applications

European Award	UK Award
Rank Xerox (1992)	ICL High Performance Technology (1995)
Design to Distribution (1994)	Ulster Carpet Mills (1996)
Texas Instruments (1995)	Mortgage Express (1996)
Brisa (1996)	
SGS - Thomson (1997)	
TNT (UK) (1998)	

Externally, a growing number of partnerships and networks exist to share the results of self assessment against award frameworks, and indeed, EFQM and BQF have encouraged the establishment of groups and working parties interested in specific criteria within the Model.

EFQM and BQF also publish anonymous data on the range of scores achieved by award applicants. These are presented cumulatively to protect identification of individual applicants, but by making a few simple arithmetical assumptions it is easy to infer that award-winners and prize-winners in the European Award process are now achieving scores in the 700-800 point band. The data also show that best practice performance for most individual criteria tends to score in 70-80% band, with very isolated examples of performance at the 80-90% level.

To create a vision of excellence and a common language to achieve it

"The further you go into the quality improvement process, the more you realise you'll never get there. If you think you've arrived, you're going downhill"

-Roger Milliken

The stretching nature of the Business Excellence Model, and the fact that it moves ever forward as best practice develops, rather than remaining a static standard, make it an ideal aspirational target. Many organisations set themselves goals of a given score against the Model, or aim for a minimum score improvement in the coming year(s). Our experience with award-winning companies suggests that an annual score increase of 100 points is possible. However, as overall scores increase towards 500 points and beyond, a sustained increase of 50 points each year is a significant challenge. Winning companies are extensively profiled in print, and there are many opportunities to hear their managers speak at, for example, winners' conferences. In addition, most will host visits for other organisations to share their approach. This means that the organisation wishing to learn has many opportunities to expose its staff, at all levels, to winning organisations.

To achieve winning levels of performance requires the efforts of everyone in the company to be aligned with the goal. One great value of the Business Excellence Model is to provide a common terminology and language for everyone in the business. This can be a key step in creating a 'constancy of purpose' which ensures that organisations do not flit from one initiative to another, but instead keep an enduring focus on the goal.

To respond more effectively to customer requirements

"The single most important thing to remember about any enterprise is that results exist only on the outside. The result of a business is a satisfied customer. The result of a hospital is a healed patient. The result of a school is a student who has learned something and puts it to work ten years later. Inside an enterprise there are only costs"

-Peter Drucker

The results of an assessment against the Model provide a useful analysis of a company's capability, and this can be a powerful tool in convincing potential customers to buy products and services. Several leading exponents of Business Excellence are starting to require their suppliers to use the Model, part of their thinking being that this will encourage the supplier to adopt proven, systematic approaches, and to drive for continuous improvement. While similar claims can be made for certification to, for example, ISO 9000, the Business Excellence Model provides a much more extensive picture of capability. With the increased focus on partnerships in the improved Model, we expect to see many more examples of this in the future.

To gain public recognition by winning awards

Winning the European award, or a national or regional equivalent, is a major achievement. Yet relatively few organisations will reach this level, and so enhance their reputation and image. Several serious contestants for the awards have had the foresight to consider what winning might mean for the organisation's improvement process. Will winning provide an additional spur to improvement, or will it encourage complacency? Most conclude that it will provide welcome recognition of what is often a long, and increasing tough, improvement journey. But they are equally sure that striving for further improvement starts again the next day, or as soon as the feedback report from the award assessors arrives.

"People seldom improve when they have no model but themselves to copy after"

-Oliver Smith playwright

The feedback from an application takes the form of a report, prepared by the assessor team, containing detailed strengths and areas for improvement, for each criterion part of the Model, together with score bands at overall and criterion level. This is supplemented by an overview, or executive summary, which draws out the key improvement themes running through the whole application.

Perhaps the most telling message comes from those organisations who have won an award at the second, third, or even fourth attempt. They say that the feedback from their earlier, unsuccessful application(s) significantly increased, and in some cases doubled, the pace of improvement in their company.

In addition, many organisations apply for an award with no expectation of winning, or even of being a finalist. They want the benefit of independent assessment by a team of trained assessors, at a modest cost. Alastair Kelly, Managing Director of 1994 European Award winners D2D called this 'the best and cheapest consultancy you can get'. Within the organisation, the independence of this feedback ensures that it is taken seriously, and an application for an award can be a major step in convincing doubting managers of the value of Business Excellence.

To make inter-site and inter-divisional comparisons

"Companies are normally unable to move in a new direction across a broad front. Instead they move in single file; one division after another, one department after another. This tends to be true even if there has been an upper-management mandate requiring all to move."

-Joseph Juran

Ranked last in our survey, this practice involves the use of business excellence assessments to compare divisions within a company and to stimulate best practice sharing and an element of internal competition.

This area has seen increasing interest in recent years, with several major organisations, for example BT and Rolls-Royce, introducing internal awards based on Business Excellence assessments. In addition, the increasing frequency of corporate mergers and acquisitions has given an opportunity to compare the approaches of the individual partners, and examples of companies using Business Excellence in this way are Lloyds TSB and Glaxo Wellcome.

The benefits of internal comparisons far outweigh any potential negative aspects. That said, organisations to need to balance internal competition with the recognition that the 'real' competition is out there in the marketplace.

Conclusions

It is apparent that organisations initially adopt Business Excellence in order to get an understanding of what they are good at, and where they can improve. In many cases, there are areas of the Model where the organisation may have no recognised process at all, and this initial assessment identifies where these need to be put in place. In addition, the first assessment may also reveal a score that challenges existing perceptions of where the organisation ranks in excellence terms. This can provide a humbling, and therefore powerful, stimulus to improve.

As their confidence grows, and they can demonstrate some successes, their thoughts turn from internal process improvement to comparing and matching performance with others. They adopt a variety of approaches to encourage development of a competitive spirit, including participation in both internal and external competition.

Making organisation-wide improvements cannot be achieved by ad-hoc, anecdotal approaches. Using the Business Excellence Model as the framework for the organisation's strategic planning process can bring major benefits in providing a holistic process and language which aligns everyone in the organisation with its goals and strategies.

Chapter Four:

Gaining Commitment

Business Excellence is a holistic approach to managing for improvement, and so is most successful when it has the full support of everyone in the organisation. To reach this point requires development and implementation of a systematic plan to raise awareness and understanding, deal with any barriers, and gradually build the support of the key players in the organisation.

A common starting point is reached when one person, often - but not necessarily -a member of the executive team, attends a conference, hears a speaker or reads about Business Excellence. The task is then to get the subject onto the executive agenda.

Raising awareness

There are a number of ways to raise the awareness of the team. These can include:

- Providing reading materials, such as those published by EFQM and BQF;
- Circulating copies of a published award-winning submission (the more recent the better);
- Preparing a presentation on how the Model might relate to the organisation.

These might be good starting points if the person trying to gain commitment is not in the executive team. While organisations have done all of these as a first step, it appears that higher levels of impact are achieved when there is an opportunity to meet face-to face with executives and/or organisations who have already been using the Model for some time. Approaches might include inviting an executive of an organisation using the Model to speak to your executive team, visiting excellent organisations, getting people involved in a network of excellent companies, or attending conferences.

Peer group speakers

This is potentially a very powerful method of raising awareness. Executives from award-winning companies are expected to share their learning, and may do this by hosting visits to their own facilities. Alternatively, you can invite someone to meet your executive team, perhaps in an evening, to be followed by dinner, to allow for informal discussions. If the organisation you have approached to share its knowledge is a significant supplier to your business, there is the opportunity for benefit for both parties. Your major IT, logistics, or telecomms supplier might be a good choice, or there may be a well-regarded organisation in your supply chain.

Visits to excellent organisations

There is no substitute for seeing excellence in action, and one powerful mechanism to gain commitment is to ask each member of the executive team to identify and visit an excellent company within the next couple of months, and set up a special executive meeting to share learning.

If it proves difficult to identify appropriate organisations, there are several ways to move forward. Joining EFQM or BQF provides access to a wide range of organisations, through common interest groups, and there are commercial best practice and benchmarking clubs in the UK.

Also in the UK, there is the 'Inside UK Excellence' programme, where, for a nominal fee, individuals and groups can visit organisations in the programme for a day. These organisations will often tailor the programme to meet special interests identified in advance.

Involvement in networks

You may wish to get involved in an existing network of practitioners to get an understanding of the current practice of Business Excellence in your industry. The common interest groups, referred to above, may be a good starting point. Alternatively, you may wish to take a broader perspective, and join a group with a common interest in Business Excellence, but without any industry bias. If so, BQC runs BESAN, the Business Excellence Self-Assessment Network. If interested, contact details are provided at the end of this book.

Conferences

Conferences can be helpful, but choose with care, given that this is now an industry in itself. The EFQM 'learning edge' conference, and the BQF/EFQM award winners' conferences, can always be recommended, but these are essentially annual events. In the UK, the regional award sponsors are now starting to run winners' conferences, and experience to date suggests that these are a good starting point for organisations relatively new to Business Excellence, who want to meet others in a similar position, as well as hear from some role model organisations.

Moving into action

Once everyone in the team has some awareness, the organisation needs to define why, and if, it should aim for excellence. This needs to be a debate at a very fundamental level, including an assessment of what might happen if the organisation decides not to adopt excellence at present, how the organisation might need to change, and what the 'agenda for action' might be.

Assuming the outcome of this debate is in favour of adopting Business Excellence, the next step is to decide how to move forward. One of the most powerful ways to experience the potential of Business Excellence is to carry out an assessment of the organisation; not only does this bring the Model to life, it also provides the organisation with a foundation for all its subsequent improvement work.

The next Chapter therefore reviews the various ways in which an initial assessment can be carried out.

Chapter Five:

Carrying out the first assessment

Introduction

An organisation that has gained the commitment to carry out a first assessment has a number of options to choose from.

In order of increasing rigour, these include: -

- Simple, questionnaire-based assessments;

- Facilitated workshops based on participants' perceptions;

- Facilitated workshops based on previously gathered information;

- Creation and assessment of Award-style submission documents.

All of these can be valuable and worthwhile approaches. The most appropriate choice will depend on factors such as the amount of time available, the extent to which the organisation is happy to rely on people's opinions, and whether a score is required or not. As an award-style submission is unlikely to be the choice for a first assessment, we will cover the creation and assessment of award-style submission documents later, in Chapter Seven.

EFQM has surveyed its members to determine which approaches are most commonly used (see Diagram 5.1)

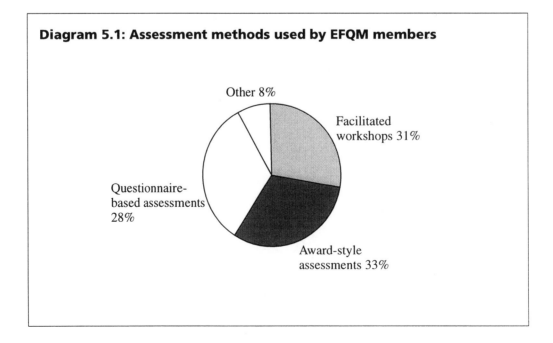

Diagram 5.1: Assessment methods used by EFQM members

Other 8%

Facilitated workshops 31%

Questionnaire-based assessments 28%

Award-style assessments 33%

Questionnaire-based approaches

There are a growing number of questionnaire- or matrix-based approaches that can be used to conduct a simple first assessment. The most straightforward of these is possibly the one-page business improvement matrix.

Diagram 5.2: Business Improvement Matrix (sample)

	Leadership	Policy & Strategy	People Management	Resources	Processes	Customer Satisfaction	People Satisfaction	Impact on Society	Business Results
10	All managers are proactive in sustaining continuous improvement.	Mission and business policy statements cover the whole business, and everyone understands them.	All actions are directed towards realising the full potential of all employees.	The organisation's resources are deployed effectively to meet policy and strategy objectives.	Key value added processes are understood, formally managed and continuously improved.	There is a positive trend in customer satisfaction. Targets are being met. There are some benchmarking targets across the industry.	Regular comparison with external companies show employee satisfaction is comparable with other companies and has improving trends.	Views of local society are proactively canvassed. Results are fed back into the companies and has improving trends.	There are consistent trends of improvement in 50% of key results areas. Some results are clearly linked to approach.
9	Managers are able to demonstrate their external involvement in the promotion of Total Quality as a business philosophy based on their own experience.	A process is in place to analyse competitor business strategy and modify unit plans as a result in order to develop and sustain a competitive advantage.	Employees are empowered to run their business processes.	A process is in place to identify additional resources which can be used to strengthen competitive advantage.	The existence of a formal quality management system can be demonstrated.	75% of customer satisfaction targets are being met.	Results indicate that employees and their families feel integrated into the work environment.	Benchmarking has started for 25% of impact on society targets.	All targets are being met and showing continuous improvement in 25% of trends.
8	Managers have a consistent approach towards continuous improvement across the unit.	The policy and strategy process are benchmarked.	The Human Resource plan for the unit supports the company's policy and strategy for continuous improvement.	A system is in place to review and modify the allocation of resources based on changing business needs.	Process performance is demonstrably linked to customer requirements.	50% of customer satisfaction targets are being met.	Results indicate that people feel valued for their contribution at work.	50% of impact on society targets are being met.	75% of targets have been achieved. Able to demonstrate relevance of key results areas to business.
7	etc	etc	etc.............						

This offers a set of nine ten-point scales, one for each criterion of the Model, with a phrase to allow the assessor to locate the organisation's current level of achievement. Of increasing sophistication are the EFQM and BQF products 'Determining Business Excellence' and 'Assess' respectively. These are based on a set of around one hundred questions, and then use the responses to develop a score.

BQC has developed a questionnaire-based approach called 'The Business Driver'. For each criterion of the Model, this asks users to rate their organisations, against a set of questions, using a simple five-point scale (see Diagram 5.3).

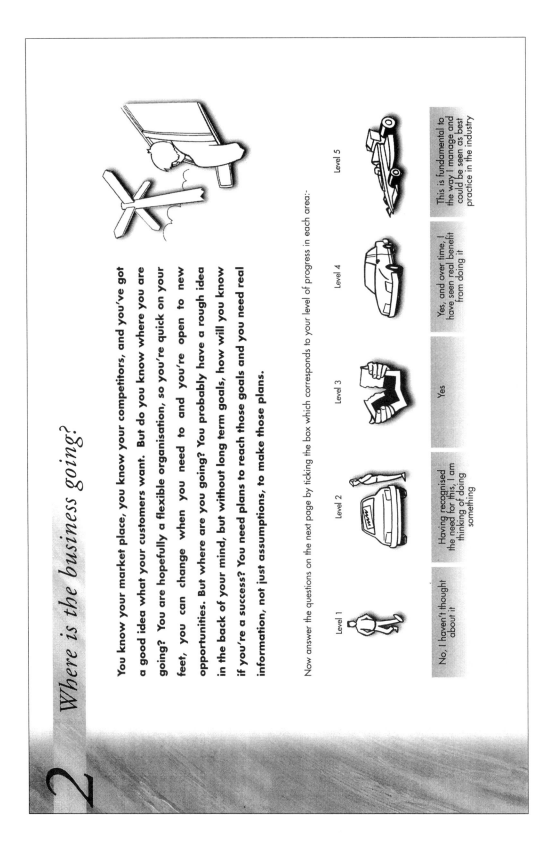

2 Where is the business going?

You know your market place, you know your competitors, and you've got a good idea what your customers want. But do you know where you are going? You are hopefully a flexible organisation, so you're quick on your feet, you can change when you need to and you're open to new opportunities. But where are you going? You probably have a rough idea in the back of your mind, but without long term goals, how will you know if you're a success? You need plans to reach those goals and you need real information, not just assumptions, to make those plans.

Now answer the questions on the next page by ticking the box which corresponds to your level of progress in each area:-

Level 1	Level 2	Level 3	Level 4	Level 5
No, I haven't thought about it	Having recognised the need for this, I am thinking of doing something	Yes	Yes, and over time, I have seen real benefit from doing it	This is fundamental to the way I manage and could be seen as best practice in the industry

Diagram. 5.3: The Business Driver approach to assessing policy and strategy

Where is the business going?

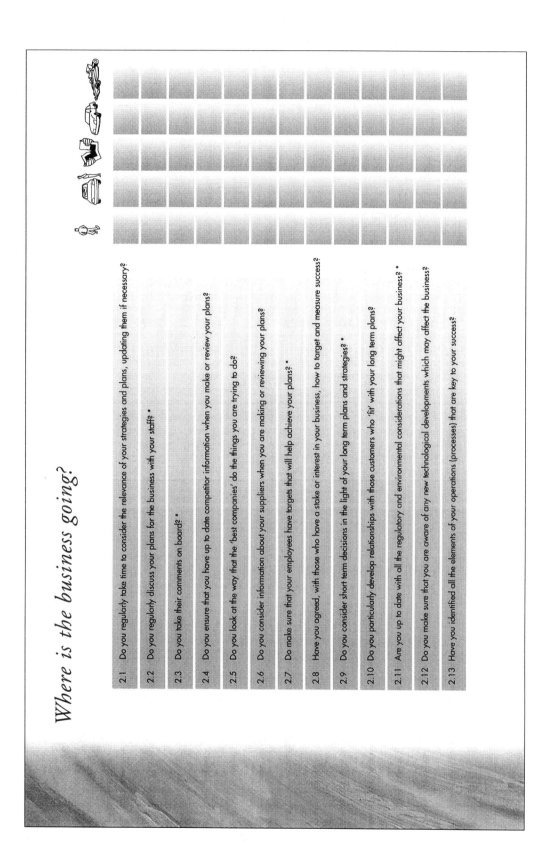

2.1 Do you regularly take time to consider the relevance of your strategies and plans, updating them if necessary?

2.2 Do you regularly discuss your plans for the business with your staff? *

2.3 Do you take their comments on board? *

2.4 Do you ensure that you have up to date competitor information when you make or review your plans?

2.5 Do you look at the way that the 'best companies' do the things you are trying to do?

2.6 Do you consider information about your suppliers when you are making or reviewing your plans?

2.7 Do you make sure that your employees have targets that will help achieve your plans? *

2.8 Have you agreed, with those who have a stake or interest in your business, how to target and measure success?

2.9 Do you consider short term decisions in the light of your long term plans and strategies? *

2.10 Do you particularly develop relationships with those customers who 'fit' with your long term plans?

2.11 Are you up to date with all the regulatory and environmental considerations that might affect your business? *

2.12 Do you make sure that you are aware of any new technological developments which may affect the business?

2.13 Have you identified all the elements of your operations (processes) that are key to your success?

The responses can then be used to develop a consensus within the team of the organisation's relative strengths and areas for improvement. 'The Business Driver' also contains questions that can be posed to other members of the organisation to test that the assessor team has a true picture of the whole organisation.

Originally developed to provide a simple entry point to Business Excellence for small organisations, 'The Business Driver' has also been particularly successful in divisions and business units of large organisations. In addition, it has been deployed across all districts of the UK in a major public sector initiative to enhance employment prospects for young people.

Facilitated perception workshops

A more rigorous approach to assessing Business Excellence, which is intended to ensure strong ownership of the output, is the perception-based workshop. With this approach, the executive team in a company comes together in a workshop environment to undertake a 'live' assessment over a one to one-and-a-half day period.

During the workshop, the team compiles lists of strengths and areas for improvement against each of the elements of the framework, based on their current perceptions. With appropriate facilitation, the team members can be prompted to ensure that they have addressed all the relevant areas. This facilitation also needs to provide some external calibration (and possibly moderation also!) to arrive at a consensus score for each item or sub-criterion within the chosen model.

The whole model can be addressed in one workshop, and there is an advantage in the team seeing their entire company against the model in one exercise. However, if more time is needed to discuss the issues, the model can be addressed in sections over a series of meetings.

This can prove to be a particularly effective process, provided that the group is strongly facilitated. The key challenge is to identify what is crucial to the assessment from a mass of thoughts of varying relevance, and we recommend that an event of this type is run by two experienced facilitators. The BQC publication 'The Facilitator's Support Kit' by Steve Bratt and Hugh Gallacher (ISBN 1-902169-05-0) gives detailed guidance on how all these workshops can be run successfully.

Facilitated workshops based on previously gathered information

There is, of course, no guarantee that the perceptions of the executive team are an accurate representation of the organisation, though one would certainly hope that it was so. In order to avoid problems of this sort, the organisation may choose to take a further step and carry out an assessment based on data.

For this workshop, members of the team first attend an awareness session to build their understanding of the Model and its requirements. At this session, typically lasting between half a day and a full day, they are given individual assignments to gather data relevant to one or more criteria within the Model, and shape it into 'strengths' and 'areas for improvement'. The team reconvenes once all the data is gathered, and gatherers present their data for the whole team to debate, amend and score.

In appendix 2 of this book there is a complete set of proformas, which lead data gatherers in a step-by-step way to identify all the information they will need for the workshop.

Because the thoughts are already filtered and ordered, this is a more straightforward workshop to facilitate, and can generally be managed by one facilitator in one day. There is also the opportunity to create a credible, high-value output, provided that sufficient effort is put into data gathering. A point is reached however, when the value of additional data gathering is limited by the workshop constraints. When this point is reached, an award-style submission starts to become the most appropriate assessment mechanism.

One of the major benefits of workshop-based assessments is the direct involvement of senior management. This involvement invariably results in the development of several strong champions of Business Excellence. In addition, it is intensive, and focused on outputs, and meaningful strategic plans can be created in little more than a day.

A potential disadvantage of the workshop-based assessment is that it tends to result in a score that is higher than that obtained from an award-style submission. While we would be among the first to claim that the profile of relative strengths and areas for improvement is of far more value than a score, it can compromise the credibility of the Model in organisations that use both assessment methods. A simple solution is to be aware of the potential issue, and to use an effective facilitating approach with enough challenge to ensure that the score is credible when tested against the intent of the RADAR card.

Chapter Six:

Action Planning

Once an initial internal assessment is completed, the organisation will have gathered a long list of strengths and areas for improvement.

One chief executive referred to this list as 'an explosion of opportunities'. But how should these be managed? The thought of having this challenge can be a major barrier to carrying out an assessment against the Model, and few managers are comfortable with the idea of creating more potential work than the organisation can sustain.

The answer lies in a systematic approach to prioritisation and action.

The BQC approach

Based on practices in award winning companies, such as Texas Instruments and others, we have evolved an approach to managing and prioritising large numbers of areas for improvement. The first step is to identify the impact of the various sub-criteria, and then to map impact against assessment performance.

Step One: The Impact Matrix

The starting point is to decide which of the sub-criteria of the Model have the most impact on the organisation. If you have used the proformas in appendix 2 of this book to gather data, the first question on each proforma will have already prompted you to answer this question. The sub-criteria should each be ranked on an impact scale of say:-

    0 = not a key issue
    1 = moderately important
    2 = important
    3 = critical

To ensure that the organisation gives sufficient thought to this ranking, we suggest that each of the four impact scores be given to no more than ten sub-criteria.

The internal assessment will also have identified a score for each sub-criterion. The next step is to plot the impact, and the score on a two-axis matrix. The horizontal axis should run from 0%, on the left, to the highest sub-criterion score you have recorded in the assessment, on the right. This should be bisected by the vertical axis at the halfway point.

This plot will populate all four segments. The bottom left segment is populated with low scoring items of low impact. Clearly you will want to improve these scores at some point, but they are not a priority. We refer to these as 'backburner' issues. On the bottom right, there are low-impact, high-scoring parts. We suggest that these are not a priority either, but in this case are potentially a fertile source of resources to deal with more important issues. In the top right, there are high impact, high scoring parts. These are your sources of strength, and should be reinforced, we suggest by continuous improvement.

The 'vital few' areas for improvement are in the top left quadrant. These are of high impact on the business, but are scoring at a low level.

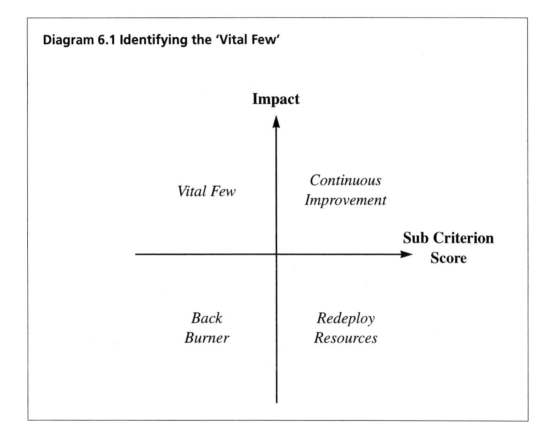

Diagram 6.1 Identifying the 'Vital Few'

By this simple process, we have focused attention on the most important sub-criteria. By forcing the organisation to use all the 'Impact' scale, this will have highlighted perhaps eight sub-criteria. From the assessment, each of these will typically have about five associated areas for improvement.

To filter this further, we now need to return to the assessment and identify the two most important areas for improvement from each of the eight sub-criteria. This is a sufficiently small number to do as a team, and it is important that the team does it, rather than sub-contract it to individuals. The next step is to tease out the underlying issues by using an affinity diagram.

Step Two: The Affinity Diagram

Each of these important areas for improvement should be written on a 'post-it' note, and the whole set stuck on a large board or wall. These should be grouped, or clustered, by the team. It is helpful to do this in silence, and then to discuss them once the clustering is complete.

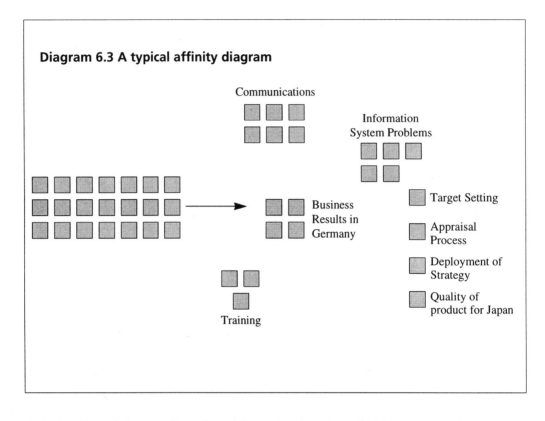

Diagram 6.3 A typical affinity diagram

This should result in a small number of focused actions that will address many of the priority issues raised by the assessment. However, the fact that these areas scored relatively lowly, yet were of high impact on the business, suggests that they are intractable problems, and addressing them may be a challenge. These could easily take up all the available improvement effort. To make some more rapid progress, it is therefore helpful to identify some 'quick wins'.

Step Three: The Impact / Ease assessment

We suggest that you return to the remaining areas for improvement in the sub-criteria in the 'vital few' segment of Diagram 6.2, and conduct a second clustering exercise. For each cluster, give it a score for its impact on the business, and a score for how easy it will be to tackle, using the following guide: -

IMPACT	EASE OF ADDRESSING
4 = Significant Impact	4 = Easy
3 = Very Beneficial	3 = Readily Achievable
2 = Some Benefit	2 = Considerable Effort
1 = Little Impact	1 = Extremely difficult

For each cluster, multiply the impact and ease scores together and focus on those with the higher number. Pick a small number of these and build them into your plan as 'quick wins'

Integrating action into the planning cycle

After a first assessment, an organisation will have to decide whether to integrate the 'vital few' and the 'quick wins' with the existing set of priorities, or whether to run Business Excellence as a 'project' for a little while.

In practice, this is often an evolutionary process. Many organisations start with a 'Business Excellence project' in order to satisfy themselves of its value, and to learn more, before integrating it into the existing planning cycle.

If the organisation chooses a project-based approach, it is often helpful to create a project steering team. This should have senior management representation to ensure that it has a voice at the executive table, and should comprise sufficient people to cover all the criteria of the Model. In practice, it is also highly desirable for the steering team to have undergone assessor training, so that they can act as experts throughout the business. The role of the project steering team may include

- creating, and managing, the overall Business Excellence project plan;
- raising awareness of Business Excellence throughout the organisation;
- training staff as assessors;
- facilitating and co-ordinating improvement projects;
- facilitating assessments;
- reporting on progress.

It may be that the senior management team of the organisation decides, at some point, to integrate Business Excellence into the planning cycle, and, indeed, to make it the framework for the way in which it manages the business. If this is the case, it is inevitable that the senior team will become the champions of excellence.

Many organisations choose to do this by appointing 'criterion owners' round the executive table. A 'criterion owner' then becomes accountable for the overall approach to that criterion, and is a sponsor for improvements designed to improve that criterion. Invariably, the managing director or chief executive officer becomes the owner of 'leadership', the finance director or controller becomes the owner of 'key performance results', the operations or production director owns 'processes' and the HR director ends up with 'people' and 'people results'. This is probably the most common approach, and, from the viewpoint of relevant expertise, is entirely appropriate. However, it may be worthy of further thought, particularly if the organisation wishes to encourage more broad, and general, management skills rather than functional leadership.

One option is to allocate ownership of criteria outside the individual executive's specialism, though in practice this tends to look 'artificial' and can challenge accountabilities.

A more appropriate response perhaps, (and adopted by a leading global pharmaceutical manufacturer) is to place criterion ownership at the management tier below the executive level, with a group of 'rising stars', and for the appropriate functional executive to provide mentoring to that person. These 'rising stars' report formally to the executive group, who take collective responsibility for the overall programme, while at the same time having the opportunity to see, and assess, the next generation of executives at work.

Whichever mechanism is chosen, it becomes appropriate to align internal assessments - and external assessments (for example, the various award processes) if possible - with the organisation's planning cycle. To leave sufficient time for assessment reports to be created, and digested after the assessment, we suggest that the assessment itself occurs at least two months before the key planning event.

Chapter Seven:

Assessment using award - style submissions

Introduction

Creation of an award-style submission is perhaps the most challenging internal assessment mechanism, but probably, in turn, yields the greatest benefits.

For an internal assessment, the organisation can adopt any format it chooses. However, once an organisation has created, assessed and scored an award-style submission, it often decides to seek external, and independent, calibration by entering the submission for one of the Award schemes. It is therefore good practice to abide by the rules of the various Award processes from the start.

The assessing bodies lay down detailed requirements to ensure equality between all applicants. These include limiting the length of the overall document to no greater than seventy-five pages, and specifying the minimum font size that is to be used.

Creating an award-style submission is covered in detail in the BQC publication 'The Submission Writer's Handbook' by Mike Parry (ISBN 1-902169-03-4). In this book we intend to give a short summary of the key steps. First, we examine the creation of an award-style submission, then consider internal assessment of this document, and finally, look at external assessment by submitting the submission for an Award.

Creating an award-style submission

Planning

Companies producing award-style submissions typically form a cross-functional team to manage the project, gather the data required, and take the submission through various drafts to its final form.

The most effective project management approach is to appoint an overall owner of the whole submission document, supported by individual criterion leaders. Each of these criterion leaders should be supported by a data gathering team and a writer. Experience has shown that all team members need to have a good understanding of the Model, for example, by being trained as assessors. This will help the team to get 'inside' the mind of the assessors, so that they understand how to present their company in a way that will lead to a fair reflection of its current position. The writers also need this training, and of course also need the skills to express complex issues clearly and succinctly in writing. Initially, it is likely that different people will write the individual criteria, particularly for an internal assessment. If the submission is to be entered for an external Award, it will add value for one individual to edit the entire document to create a more consistent overall style. Internal copywriters can usefully perform this role, if you have them.

CHESTER COLLEGE WARRINGTON LIBRARY

It is essential to create a project plan, covering data gathering, drafting each criterion part, and review. It is inevitable that there will be a number of drafts, and it is easy to lose track of updated material unless there is some element of version control. A simple system, such as that used to maintain controlled documents such as quality system procedures, is valuable to prevent many versions of the same document being in circulation.

Creating an award-style submission can take as long as you are prepared to give it. However, a typical project plan could see a first draft being available after 7-8 weeks, a reviewed and refined second draft after 13-14 weeks, and a formally accepted and signed-off document after sixteen weeks.

Scope and key themes - two essential steps

Right at the start of the project, it is essential to scope the assessment by defining the boundaries of the organisation to be assessed.

It may be, for example, that the organisation is a division or sub-unit within a larger enterprise, with full accountability for some of its activities, but taking some of its internal services from the parent company.

It may have a core of permanent staff, complemented with short-contract agency staff to cope with seasonal fluctuations in demand. Or, it may contract out non-core activities to another organisation, but have that organisation's people on its sites, and therefore have some responsibility for their health and safety. A decision needs to be made on whether these people are considered as employees or suppliers.

Next, it needs to consider who the customers are. While the end customer will usually be clear, the parent company may form an intermediary step in the customer chain. When we talk of 'customer' it is essential that we share the same understanding.

Then it is appropriate to consider other stakeholders, for example the shareholders, but possibly also any regulatory bodies who may influence, and can in principle control, some aspects of the organisation's operations.

Next it should consider which community stakeholders are affected by its operations. These will usually include the local community around its operating sites, but may include pressure groups, local politicians, and some national or international bodies.

Once these various relationships are defined, it is important that everyone involved in creating the document has a common understanding. Without this, there is potential for major confusion. A simple 'ring fence' diagram (see Diagram 7.1) should be developed and made available to all.

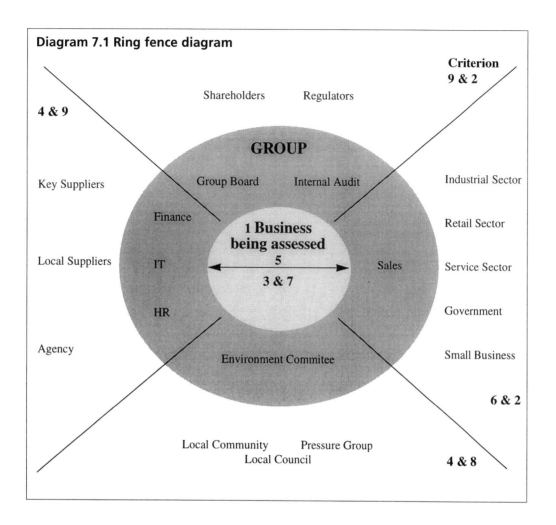

Diagram 7.1 Ring fence diagram

Criterion
9 & 2

4 & 9

Shareholders   Regulators

GROUP

Key Suppliers

Group Board   Internal Audit

Industrial Sector

Finance

Retail Sector

1 Business being assessed
5
3 & 7

Local Suppliers

IT

Sales

Service Sector

HR

Government

Agency

Environment Commitee

Small Business

6 & 2

Local Community   Pressure Group
Local Council

4 & 8

Also at the start, it is helpful for the executive team to identify the 'key themes' that they would like the submission to project. These are the handful of points that describe the positive attributes of the organisation - really a thumbnail sketch of its distinctive features. As with the ring fence, these should be communicated to all involved, in order to focus data gathering on the critical issues.

Data gathering

There is usually no shortage of data in most organisations, and so the key to success is focusing on that which is relevant and supportive to the assessment.

The data collected needs to be relevant to: -

- The key points in the history of the company
- The key themes
- The Business Excellence criteria
- The RADAR card criteria
- Deployment of the approach
- Links between individual criteria

The sources of potentially useful data are many and varied. The people or unit responsible for management information, performance data, corporate reporting, budgets and forecasts, should be your first port of call. Also use this visit to identify where historical data is likely to be located. Often, material concerning previous years will be archived, and you may want to find data relating to five or more years ago.

Quality and process manuals and procedures can be fertile sources, particularly for the process diagrams that will help you to describe many of the enabling approaches.

Minutes of executive meetings, and any associated performance reports, can be useful in identifying why performance has varied. This can be helpful in explaining trends in 'results' criteria.

Look also at less formal sources - for example, company notice boards, press coverage, and PR departments. These can often be useful sources of 'society results'.

And finally, there is a vast amount of priceless data in the heads of the employees. Talking to a wide cross-section of staff will provide the many examples that give your submission authenticity and a 'human' feel.

In collecting data, you should recognise that what you find may also be helpful to other criteria. For that reason it is helpful to devise a standard pro-forma to ensure that data can be traced to its original source.

In sharing data across criteria, it may be helpful to create matrices showing where in the submission key organisational activities will be described. For example, the annual performance appraisal will probably have most impact in criterion three, but will also have some impact in criteria one, two, seven, and possibly others. Creation of these matrices will help prevent duplication of material in several criteria.

Writing the submission

As data begins to flow in, it is time to start creating the first draft. First, the writers need to be given some indication of the space they have available. If it is likely that the submission will eventually be submitted to one of the Award processes, then it is essential to meet the maximum limit of seventy-five pages.

As a starting brief, space should be allocated on the basis of the points available in the Model. It is common to find a submission starting with a brief overview of the organisation, covering not more than three pages. The remaining pages are then allocated on a pro-rata basis as follows: -

Overview	3 pages
Leadership	7 pages
Policy and strategy	6 pages
People	7 pages
Resources	7 pages
Processes	10 pages
Customer results	14 pages
People results	6 pages
Society results	4 pages
Key performance results	11 pages

These should be regarded as guidelines rather than absolutes, but it is a good starting discipline. Once the document is approximately the right size, it may be appropriate to give relatively more space to criteria relating to the key themes or where performance is strong. (Review of recent Award-winning documents also suggests that they give rather more space to the 'enabler' criteria than the table above might suggest.)

In the initial stages, it is helpful to concentrate simply on the overall content. Diagrams, charts and graphs can be hand drawn until the final draft; creating these by computer at an early stage can often be a poor use of time.

It is helpful to create a sub-team within the project and make it accountable for the links between criteria. The Model requires links to be made in many areas, and this team should help the criterion owners put these in place. In addition, this team is in a good position to review linking criteria for overlaps and inconsistencies.

Production standards

Award entrants produce reports of varying production quality. It is not necessary to produce a highly glossy report, and indeed some award assessors are put off by overly expensive presentation. The key is to make the material clear, easy to read and cross-reference, and to ensure that the text is written in a relaxed, easy to read style.

The next decision to make is to choose an overall page structure. Although award applicants have experimented with various formats, one of the most flexible is to use portrait orientation with two columns of text.

Graphs in particular should be sufficiently large to make the message clear. Although it adds to the production cost, use of different colours is more distinctive than different black line styles.

Experiment with typeface and select the one that gives the cleanest and clearest look to a number of people.

Many organisations use page dividers to separate the individual criteria. Custom and practice suggests that it is acceptable to include visual material, for example photographs of locations, people and products on these dividers, but not to include text. Text will then make these dividers part of the seventy-five pages.

Assessors appreciate a cover which is hard wearing and is easily laid flat. Choose a paper which will accept highlighter pen inks - many assessors use a colour coded set of highlighters to mark 'strengths' 'areas for improvement' and 'site visit issues'.

Advantages and disadvantages of award-style submissions

Basing an internal assessment on an award-style process creates the advantage of knowing that a well-tested yardstick is being used. The fact that many others are using it allows you to make some direct comparisons with the results of others through benchmarking and self-assessment networks.

The detailed nature of the data gathering and the collating process ensures sufficient depth to give an accurate judgement of the company. This consistency is further enhanced by training those involved to the same level as that of the award assessors. This approach also opens up the opportunity of applying for an award and receiving a formal feedback report from the award administrators.

The disadvantages in using the award-style submission approach relate mainly to a potential danger that senior managers are not sufficiently involved in creating and assessing the submission to feel strong ownership. It is essential that their involvement extends at least to signing-off the submission as a fair and accurate reflection of the organisation. This ensures that the raw material for the assessment is adequately validated. To build the integrity of the assessment process, it is desirable for a representative of the senior management team to play an assessor role, or at least to sit in on the assessors' consensus discussions.

Internal assessment of the submission

Once an internal submission has been completed, an assessor team must be established. It is highly desirable for this team to include some external experts, and these can be found either from consultancy organisations like BQC or from sister companies. Many organisations choose assessor teams comprising a mix of internal and external staff, and this can be ideal in striking a balance between knowledge of the organisation and external expertise and independence. This mixed approach also helps to develop understanding within the organisation, while maintaining a strong sense of local ownership for the outputs.

A typical team would comprise four to six assessors. All of these should be trained using the calibrated case studies that form part of the training for the European and national Award assessors. In this way, companies can ensure an internal consistency in the assessment process.

Ideally, a balanced team is needed. As a general rule it will include members from different functions, with different backgrounds and experiences. Above all, it should offer as rounded a view of corporate excellence as possible. As part of the assessment, it may be appropriate to undertake the equivalent of an award 'site visit'. This can be used to clarify and verify some of the issues raised by the report and to give the organisation an experience of how a site visit feels. Alternatively, some companies arrange for their assessors to meet with the submission writers to explore areas of the report that caused debate and uncertainty during the assessment.

Regardless of whether a site visit takes place, the most valuable result of the award-style assessment is the feedback report. This provides a summary of the organisation's overall strengths and areas for improvement at an overview level, and detailed sets of strengths and areas for improvement for each individual sub-criterion. Finally, it will also indicate the scoring profile of the organisation, as a measure of its progress towards excellence. Analysis of this report can provide valuable insights for the development of policy and strategy, as outlined in Chapter Six, and for identifying improvement priorities.

The feedback report in an award process highlights the applicant's position without stepping over the line of attempting to provide solutions, or telling the management team how to run their company. It is a great advantage if an internal feedback report can offer the same degree of neutrality as would be expected of an external assessor team. If this style of report can be produced successfully, it is more likely to be accepted as a fair judgement of the company against the chosen framework.

Diagram 7.2 shows a typical page from a feedback report created from an internal assessment of a leading UK pharmaceutical manufacturer.

Diagram 7.2: Feedback report extract: - 3d How people are involved, empowered and recognised

Strengths

- Every Continuous Improvement (CI) Team who complete a project make a presentation to senior management

- CI teams make presentations to external visitors

- Celebration Days take place to encourage others to join in the quality journey

- The best internal teams are chosen to compete for National Awards, eg the Michelin and Perkins Awards

- Teams and individuals are recognised at local level in various ways, for example the 'wall of achievement', 'employee of the month' etc

- Continuous improvement is planned into operating schedules rather than as ad-hoc activity

- There is a recognition system to sustain involvement and empowerment

Areas for improvement

- There is no evidence to show how managers give recognition at the CI presentations in a systematic way

- It is not clear whether the approach to involvement/empowerment is reviewed for effectiveness

- There is little evidence of the extent of celebration days

- There is some evidence to suggest that the effectiveness of the approach to empowerment is reviewed, but no indication of improvements resulting from that review

External assessment - entering for Awards

Entering for an award, whether at regional, national or European level, is a significant commitment by the organisation and its leaders. That said, the benefits can be equally significant. Entering for an award exposes the organisation to a team of independent, trained and experienced assessors, often with wide experience of senior management in major organisations. They will typically spend two or more days assessing the submission individually, and then a day or more, as a team, debating their findings and agreeing a team consensus view of the submission document.

The resulting feedback report will typically contain: -

- a description of the award process;
- an overview or executive summary;
- a set of detailed strengths and areas for improvement for each sub-criterion of the Model;
- a summary scoresheet
- anonymous data, showing how other applicants have scored against the Model.

The description of the award process is a generic section provided to all applicants.

This is followed by an overview or executive summary, which will highlight the key themes, or threads, that the assessors believe run through the application. Some assessor teams present these as stand-alone headings, while others list the most important themes in each of the nine criteria. This overview is typically two to three pages long, and provides a digestible summary suitable for tabling as a board or executive team briefing paper.

The body of the report follows, with detailed strengths and areas for improvement, presented by criterion part. Typically, each criterion part will contain four to six strengths and a similar number of areas for improvement, though clearly a high-scoring part will have more strengths and fewer areas for improvement, and vice-versa. The assessors will also have listed the most important strengths and areas for improvement at the top of the list, or have indicated these with an asterisk.

The report then presents a scoring summary. This gives a score band at criterion level; so, for example, you may know that you have scored in the 51-60% band for criterion 1,'leadership', but not what you scored for the individual sub-criteria 1a, 1b, 1c and 1d.

In addition, you receive an overall score, out of 1000 points in a 50-point band. Thus you may discover that your application scored in the band 501-550. In fact, by taking the mid-point of each of the individual criteria scores, and multiplying by the appropriate weighting, you can get a closer estimate of the most statistically likely score achieved.

Site visits

There is however another step in the award process. The assessor team will also have identified 'site visit issues', which are questions not wholly answered by the document itself. If the submission is scored above a particular level, the applicant is asked to host a site visit, where the assessor team visits the organisation, at its various locations, to resolve these site visit issues, and finalise its scoring.

Planning for a site visit

Once you receive notification that you are to receive a site visit, your organisation needs to spring into action. In fact, you may have known that a site visit was likely, from any internal assessments you have carried out, or from your performance in the previous year's award process. In that case, your planning should have started earlier.

You may wish to consider appointing a site visit project manager to co-ordinate activity. A key initial task is to contact the senior assessor and to identify his or her initial needs. There are however, a number of things you can reasonably anticipate. They will want to know: -

- Locations, and how easy it is to travel between them
- Numbers of staff and activities at each site
- Where key executives are based
- Background information on the company, for example company reports

You should have these available to send out, as an 'information pack', as soon as contact has been made.

Early in this discussion, you will want to get some sort of timetable from the senior assessor, in order for you to plan travel, hotels and to book key staff for interviews. The senior assessor will usually be willing to give you at least an outline plan to start your planning, though he or she may want to leave some flexibility, particularly towards the end of the site visit, to follow up unforeseen issues that arise during the visit. It is also legitimate to ask whether there are any particular areas of interest that the team wishes to cover. You may get only a brief outline, but nevertheless, this will be useful.

Arrange for the team to have a meeting room in your main location that they can use as a base during the visit. This should have a telephone, and it is also helpful to provide copies of documents that they will definitely want to see. These include any customer and employee survey results, and any documents or brochures that describe the company's strategies and plans. Many organisations make company videos available, to provide some useful background.

Most assessor teams want to start the visit with a meeting with the senior management team. It is very helpful to get all the senior team there, and the leader or managing director is a 'must'. These opening sessions are best kept relatively short, and ensure that there is ample opportunity for the assessors to ask questions. It is also legitimate here for the leader to ask whether there are any particular areas of interest that he or she can tackle right at the start.

After this meeting, the assessors will want to get started. You will find it valuable to assign 'hosts' to each of the assessors, so that they always have a local point of contact, and you will also know who the assessors are talking to.

Keep a record of who has met the assessors, and what the assessors were interested in. Many organisations run a daily 'wash-up' session, at the end of the day, to ensure that all unanswered questions, and material requested, are available the next morning.

Assessors will want to collect data in various ways, and a particular favourite is the 'focus group'. Identify people for these - they need to be positive enthusiastic, but above all, willing to speak up and take part in discussions.

Once the site visit team members have asked all their questions, they will want to re-score your application. Provide them with a comfortable room to do this, and leave them alone. The process forbids them from making any comment on how well you have done, so it is better not to ask. Before they leave they will want to thank you, so make sure an appropriate delegation is available to say goodbye.

Note that scores are raised as a result of the site visit in about 80% of cases!

Chapter Eight:

Best practice and case studies.

In this chapter, we are taking a slightly different approach to that followed in previous editions.

In the first part of the chapter, we present examples of best practice abstracted from the new BQC publication 'The Excellence Routefinder' by Chris Hakes (ISBN 1-902169-05-0).

These examples are intended to give the reader a flavour of how excellent organisations are currently operating, and to provoke thought on the approaches that their own organisations might adopt.

In the second part of the chapter, four leading exponents of Business Excellence are profiled. These profiles give an indication of the diversity of approaches that can be successfully adopted, and typically cover the first few years after a decision had been made to adopt Business Excellence.

1. Examples of Best Practice

'The Excellence Routefinder' is a strategic tool to enable organisations to identify a future direction and, in doing so, learn from the best practices of others. These best practices have been collected from award winners, clients, and published material over many years, and the following sections are a selection:-

Leadership

Leaders in excellent organisations:

- clearly define the mission, vision , values, objectives and plans of the organisation, division, department, unit or team;
- define appropriate leadership behaviours and standards, and deploy them across the organisation;
- measure their personal leadership effectiveness;
- visibly champion the drive for improvement, by setting simple, yet aspirational targets.

Excellent organisations:

- define clear organisational visions, values, and purposes, which engage the support of all the leadership population at all levels;
- have policies and plans to endorse training and development activities, through for example, leaders receiving training, delivering it to others, or opening and closing training courses;
- align recognition, reward, and progression to the achievement of organisational objectives and desired behaviours;

- ensure that the leadership team have a strong focus on relationships with key stakeholders such as customers, key suppliers, strategic contractors, partners, representatives of the wider community, and those with a corporate interest;
- sponsor and resource joint improvement activity with the customer to improve the quality of products or services, and to build the customer's capabilities for the future.

Policy and Strategy

Individuals in excellent organisations:

- understand what is expected of them by all their customers, suppliers and stakeholders, including the levels above them in the organisation;
- test the validity of strategy and plans with a range of informed, independent observers.

Excellent organisations:

- identify the key factors in gaining entry to new potential markets;
- adopt scenario planning techniques to assess future opportunities and risks, and to identify any necessary contingency plans;
- seek a balance between the pressures for maximising short-term financial performance, and the need for long-term sustainability;
- develop a holistic set of measures, for example, a balanced scorecard;
- identify and separate the day-to-day 'fundamental' objectives from the one-off 'breakthrough' objectives, and monitor these on different timescales if necessary;
- use a systematic goal deployment process such as 'Hoshin Kanri';
- carry out research to find out why their competitors' customers do not buy from them.

People

Leaders in excellent organisations:

- involve people at all levels in the implementation and management of change;
- foster a spirit of experimentation, innovation, and creativity, focusing on learning rather than blame;
- delegate decisions to the people with the relevant information;
- make continuous improvement of products, processes and systems a formal goal for everyone in the team;

Excellent organisations:

- design and refine organisational structures to align them with the organisation's key processes, and increase the opportunity for ownership, clear workflows, and devolved decision making;
- integrate vision, mission and value statements into all training events;
- have objectives, targets, and development plans for all employees;
- design regular organisational and individual learning opportunities, such as presentations by customers, improvement teams, and leaders from other organisations;

- ensure all presenters and briefers are trained and capable in running two - way communication sessions.
- test the reception of the message on a typical group in advance of its wholesale transmission;

Partners and Resources

Individuals in excellent organisations:

- ensure that staff are aware of the financial cost of all materials used in the organisation;
- focus part of the improvement process on eliminating waste of all kinds;
- design the workplace layout to foster employee interaction and innovation;
- give research employees time to follow their own ideas and hunches;

Excellent organisations:

- use a consistent and systematic, formal approach to project management;
- use systematic resource planning approaches;
- systematically measure and review the performance and capacity of key physical assets, for example, major production equipment;
- utilise the expertise of suppliers and partners in the design of new products and facilities;
- aspire to developing partnership relationships with statutory bodies, industry regulators, and enforcement services within the community.

Processes

Individuals in excellent organisations:

- use a focus or theme to drive process level improvement, for example, cycle time reduction, or waste elimination;
- establish a basic set of measures to monitor progress;

Excellent organisations:

- have a systematic methodology for managing their organisational processes, using multidisciplinary teams to define boundaries, content, inputs, outputs, and metrics for each identified process;
- give priority to key customer-facing processes;
- define operating standards for their processes, and use these as the basis for internal and external audits;
- establish clear goals for process innovation;
- use benchmarking, statistical variation/ process capability data, and process validation studies, to identify, prioritise, and set targets for improvement;
- involve key partners in their process thinking, identification, and design;
- use the views of customers, suppliers, auditors, experts, and other stakeholders to stimulate innovation and creativity in process management and improvement, and to identify improvement priorities;
- collaborate with other companies and academia to maximise knowledge and minimise risk.

Customer Results

Individuals in excellent organisations:

- ensure that their staff are aware of end-users, and how they value the product or service;
- identify key staff who will drive and develop customer loyalty.

Excellent organisations:

- understand what the customer values in the product or service, based on factors influencing customer loyalty;
- rank product and service features according to the needs of customers;
- set, monitor and measure customer service standards, using key differentiators of service identified by customers themselves;
- monitor the performance of competitors and best in class organisations;
- link executive remuneration to improvement in customer satisfaction;
- make use of a range of methods to obtain direct customer feedback, to avoid 'questionnaire fatigue'.

People Results

Individuals in excellent organisations:

- monitor levels of satisfaction in their own unit and set themselves personal targets;
- have personal action plans to improve satisfaction in their own area.

Excellent organisations:

- research the most important drivers of satisfaction, commitment and motivation;
- create targets for overall and individual satisfaction measures, based on benchmarks;
- compare results with direct competitors to ensure that key staff are not tempted to leave;
- segment and analyse results at a detailed level to identify any departmental/area/role trends;
- integrate people satisfaction targets into all managers' personal objectives;
- demonstrate a correlation between improving people satisfaction and other key performance measures such as customer satisfaction and business results;
- include a range of benchmark questions to enable external comparison, through organisations such as 'BEST', MORI and Gallup;
- work with working parties or commercial networks, to research best practice with other leading practitioners.

Society Results

Individuals in excellent organisations:

- set a unit or team goal related to impact on society;
- wherever possible identify potential community benefits from operational activities such as disposing of obsolete equipment, training staff, sponsoring 'fun' activities;
- set environmental objectives for some improvement activities.

Excellent organisations:

- measure and analyse press and media coverage and identify its value by comparison with advertising rates for comparable coverage and impact;
- have organisational programmes to encourage staff involvement in helping the community at large;
- encourage community service, for example as magistrates, school governors, and army reservists;
- measure and reduce the consumption of non-renewable resources through waste elimination activities;
- open their doors to the community, monitor attendance, and identify attendee perceptions by formal or informal means;
- develop links and relationships with key opinion formers, for example, local MPs, MEPs, councils, emergency services, and geographically close neighbours;
- appoint community action managers to help co-ordinate, promote and encourage community activity;
- practise good citizenship within the limits of the company's resources. Examples could include public responsibility, educational support, healthcare in the community, environmental excellence, resource conservation, community service, improving industry and business practices, and sharing of information.

Key Performance Results

Individuals in excellent organisations:

- give regular feedback to their team on business performance, and discuss its impact on the team;
- create visible displays of progress towards organisational and unit goals;
- ensure that their staff are aware of competitor performance and its potential impact.

Excellent organisations:

- use techniques such as quality function deployment to determine the relevance of key measures to stakeholders;
- identify a small set of headline measures as the organisational dashboard, which show the direction of organisational performance at a glance, and can be linked to the organisation's policy and strategy;

- cascade these headline measures as a set of linked balanced scorecards;
- regularly review the benefit that all of the measures give, and their impact on overall results;
- segment results to the lowest meaningful level in the organisation to pinpoint performance and encourage ownership;
- consider the financial investment community as a key player in influencing stakeholder value, and therefore meet regularly and openly to ensure understanding of the current situation.

2. Four profiles of success with self assessment

Although there is one Business Excellence Model, there is no one way to use it to gain benefit. The four organisations we have chosen to profile are Yellow Pages, Cleveland Constabulary, Post Office Counters Ltd., and Design to Distribution.

Yellow Pages was a European Prize Winner in 1998, Design to Distribution was the European Award Winner in 1994 and Cleveland Constabulary was a winner in the Excellence North East Award (one of the UK regional awards).

Sharing best practices is a part of the culture of excellent organisations. Each organisation profiled here has openly and enthusiastically shared its experiences, and it goes almost without saying that we are extremely grateful for the opportunity to share their learning more widely.

Business Excellence in Yellow Pages

Company profile

Yellow Pages is part of British Telecommunications plc, a major player in the global telecommunications market.

The company employs over 3,000 people in the UK and is an important player in the UK local advertising market. Each year, the company contacts over 1.7 million businesses, and publishes over 730,000 advertisements from over 350,000 of these businesses.

The products are extremely successful, with over half of the UK population using them in any given four-week period.

The core product is the Yellow Pages directory. This is published in 74 editions each year, with over 26 million copies delivered to nearly every UK home and business.

Other major products are: -
- Business Pages, a range of classified business-to-business directories;
- Talking Pages, the telephone information service;
- The Business Database, which provides information for use in direct marketing;
- YELL - an Internet information service.

Yellow Pages Quality Journey Key Steps

- Renewed focus on production quality 1985
- Total Quality training company-wide 1989/90
- Leadership development for all managers 1992/3
- ISO 9000 registration 1993
- First company Business Excellence Self Assessment 1993
- Investor in People Recognition 1997
- European Award for Business Excellence Prize Winner 1998
- ISO 14001 registration 1999

The Journey towards Excellence

Yellow Pages has a long history and successful track record in its quality journey, introducing a company-wide TQM programme in 1989, and following this with an ISO 9000 Quality Management System in 1993, and an ISO 14001 Environmental Management System in 1999. Yellow Pages first introduced award-style Business Excellence assessments in 1993. Following a second assessment in 1994, their Managing Director committed the organisation to Business Excellence with the following objective: -

'To achieve business excellence through the continuous improvement of all Yellow Pages activities by using the EFQM framework to identify strengths and areas for improvement.'

By 1995 Yellow Pages had fully integrated the Business Excellence assessment process into their annual planning cycle so that it formed a critical step in the direction setting for their business. In addition, as part of this development, the senior management team undertook full assessor training.

Key Elements of Yellow Pages Self Assessment Process

Yellow Pages complete an annual award-style submission covering the whole company. Their assessment process has the following key elements:

• Top Team Commitment

Members of the senior management team 'own' particular criteria directly relating to their areas of business responsibility. Each is responsible for leading a team to conduct an assessment and compile the data for their area.

The overall day-to-day process is managed by the Quality Management Group, who are responsible for planning and co-ordinating the approach, arranging appropriate training/awareness, ensuring linkages across criteria are addressed, handling the wider communication within the business, editing and producing the final report, and overall progress reporting to the senior team.

• Review of Self Assessment Report and Feedback

Yellow Pages award-style submissions are externally assessed to provide an independent objective assessment. In 1997, this included a site visit process. In 1998, this assessment was used to refine the document further, and to enter it in the European Award process. Yellow Pages received a Site Visit and were awarded a European Prize. In 1999, the assessment process was refined still further, and another application was made for the European Award.

• Taking Action

The assessment results and feedback are presented to the senior management team by the lead assessor. The feedback forms a key input to developing 'Top-Down Direction' for the planning period, cascading into department, team and individual objectives. As a refinement to their approach, in the 1997/8 planning cycle, Yellow Pages addressed the areas for improvement through three key avenues:

• Project teams, owned by a senior manager, were established to address six key themes. These themes were targeted at delivering improvement across all criteria, and were project managed by a steering group consisting of the same senior managers - led by the Head of Customer Services and Quality Management.

• All of the areas for improvement identified by the assessment process were allocated to the appropriate 'line' owner for review and resolution.

• The critical approaches in each enabler criterion were identified, and each was reviewed by the appropriate 'approach' owner to ensure full and effective deployment

Following their success in the European Award process in 1998, the company continued with its successful policy of criterion ownership into 1999. Part of the approach in this year was to: -

1. Target every criterion at setting the role model standard, by reference to the 1998 Award Winner's application document, and by gathering other examples of best practice.

2. Focusing, again, on ensuring high deployment of its areas of particular strength.

3. Establishing a 'links team' in addition to the Criterion teams, to ensure that the entire submission is consistent, and that all the necessary links between criteria are in place.

The benefits being obtained

The Business Excellence assessment process is providing a mechanism for consistent review and focusing of improvement activity across the whole business, through the involvement of the entire senior management team.

Key lessons

The assessment process is not static within the business. Its use to generate improvement has developed as the business and the business environment has moved forward. Although Yellow Pages has integrated the assessment process into normal practice, the process of review and refinement will also apply to the use of the model to ensure that it too is generating the best value for the business.

Future Developments

Yellow Pages are currently developing the use of Business Excellence assessment at department and team level within the business, to support the identification of local improvement initiatives, and to provide additional 'bottom-up' input to the planning process.

For further information, please contact:

Ian Adcock or Sharon Scobell
Yellow Pages
Queens Walk
Reading RG1 7PT

Business Excellence in Cleveland Constabulary

Organisation Profile

Cleveland Constabulary was established in 1974 as one of the 43 police services in England and Wales, and it is responsible for policing an area on either side of the River Tees covering some 228 square miles, with over half a million people living in both urban and rural communities. Within the force there are four operational districts and 13 operational support and central support units.

In the early 1990s the Deputy Chief Constable, in response to cost and market pressures, introduced a number of quality initiatives into the organisation. These produced some results, but were not co-ordinated, and were not generally seen as a cohesive approach to the improvement of the force. However the Business Excellence Model was perceived to be a good overall framework under which these initiatives, and others that related to the management processes of the organisation, could be drawn together.

Assessment against the Model

Training a substantial number of people as assessors was seen as key to the successful use of the Model, and self assessment, within Cleveland Constabulary. The force currently has 100 people fully trained as assessors.

The first force-wide self assessment, carried out in early 1995 after initial training, was based largely on the views of the initial group of trained assessors. All of the units within the force have completed their first self assessment using an award-style process that has involved writing unit reports for 'external' assessment, followed by action planning. In this process, the feedback has remained the property of the unit involved and only a summary has been passed to senior management. However, in practice, the units have shared their information in an effort to establish a consistent level of best practice.

However the level of time and resource required by this approach to self assessment has raised concerns. Latterly the approach has moved to one that involves a series of half-day team workshops, which are facilitated by an individual who is not member of the unit being assessed. These teams cover a range of ranks including the front line police officers. Each workshop covers the assessment of three of the model criteria, which are allocated on a rolling basis and without drawing on specific expertise. The scoring in the workshop uses the EFQM/BQF matrix. One result of the changed approach has been that an action plan is available, from the workshop, covering the expected outcomes, responsibilities, and the timescale for implementing improvements. These action plans and outcomes are now being incorporated into the annual business planning cycle.

The first full force assessment was carried out during the first half of 1997, and was externally assessed by British Steel. A steering committee has now been established to deliver the resulting action plan, and to make the preparations for a full force assessment every year.

The benefits being obtained

The process has been very well received within the force. Some of the benefits have been that:-

- Career development is linked to a practical understanding of quality concepts as they affect a particular post;
- A consistent language has been established across a mobile and widely spread workforce of 1,500 police officers and 500 civilian personnel;
- The force has been able to identify and quantify gaps and strengths in a 'no-blame' process;
- The force has been able to tailor its activities to the objectives and constraints of the organisation within the framework of the overall model and self assessment technique;
- There is an acceptance of the need to manage by fact, and not to protect your own territory at all costs;
- There is a recognition that strengths are as important as areas for improvement.

Future developments

The developments that are currently underway, or foreseen, are a recognition of the need to quantify the benefits achieved, and to relate them directly to performance measures and a quality costing model.

For further information, please contact:

Shirley Erskine
Corporate Development, Cleveland Constabulary
Police Head Quarters, P O Box 70
Ladgate Lane
Middlesborough TS8 9TH
Tel: 01642 301311

Business Excellence in Post Office Counters Ltd.

Company Profile

Post Office Counters is a wholly owned subsidiary of the Post Office Group and, with more than 19,000 outlets nation-wide and a turnover of £1,161m in 1996/97, is Britain's largest retailer. So far as we are aware, it is the first major Retail Company to undertake self assessment.

> ' *Continuous improvement is essential to allow us to move towards the 21st century with real confidence. Business Excellence Reviews and self assessment are essential parts of this improvement process. In 1996 we entered for the European Quality Award and learnt valuable lessons on the areas to improve to enable us to rub shoulders with the world's best companies. This year, we have put forward a submission for the UK Quality Award and feedback from this exercise will prove invaluable in our drive to become truly World Class'*
>
> - Stuart Sweetman, Managing Director

Self assessment

Post Office Counters' self assessment process is based on the European Model, and is known as the Business Excellence Review. The Review process is designed to minimise disruption in the Unit that is self assessed and consists of six main stages:

1. **Management Team Workshop -** a facilitated, 24 hour workshop, in which the management team of the Unit under review considers its current performance against the Business Excellence Model, produces a perceived scoring profile and prepares plans for data collection and communication within the Business Unit.

2. **Data Collection -** the Business Unit prepares a brief submission (around 30 pages) outlining current performance against the model. At the same time, questionnaires are issued to a sample of staff within the Unit. The aim of the questionnaire is to test deployment of approaches. The report and summarised questionnaire responses are then passed to the Review Team and are used to identify issues for further investigation during the site visit.

3. **Site Visit -** a review team of (usually) six assessors visits the Business Unit for three days to gather further information by means of interviews and discussion groups. The aim is to get a wide range of views from different geographical areas, different functions and different levels within the Unit. The collected data is coded against the model and analysed daily to build up a picture of the unit's strengths and areas for improvement.

4. Scoring and Judgement - the assessors then individually score the unit's performance and identify strengths and areas for improvement. A consensus discussion then takes place and the scores and the content of the feedback report to the Unit are agreed.

5. Feedback - the feedback report is sent to the Business Unit within two weeks of the Review. Within a further two weeks, a meeting between the Review Team and the Unit Management Team is held, providing an opportunity to seek clarification and more detail, if available. The content of the feedback report is confidential to the Business Unit.

6. Action planning - a feedback report provides a comprehensive description of the Business unit's current state and therefore is a valuable input to the Business Planning process. The process used for action planning and preparing the Business Plan is at the discretion of the Business Unit Leader.

Key lessons from the 1994/95 pilot were that the process worked and generated considerable interest throughout the Business. Some improvements to the materials were made and a briefing pack was introduced to help Business Units prepare for the Management Team workshop. A 'within unit' self assessment process was introduced in 1995/96. This 'within unit' process has continued to be reviewed and improved to further reduce the disruption to Units undergoing self assessment. Post Office Counters conducted self assessment reviews for all its Business Units in each of the three years up to 1996/97. These reviews have provided much useful information to the Business Units, allowing them to track their progress and compare this with the progress of Counters as a whole, with its external submissions to the BQF and EFQM.

In order to support the Business Excellence Review process, all Business Unit leaders, and the managers reporting directly to them, have been, or will be, trained as assessors. Assessor training is a two-day course, based on EFQM materials, but tailored to the Counters process, and including an outline of action planning processes.

The benefits being obtained

The major benefits of self assessment to Post Office Counters are that: -
- it provides a common framework for all units, enabling a rigorous and structured approach to business improvement;
- it provides a challenging standard for all Units in the business to work towards;
- it effectively merges the Total Quality process (Customer First) into Business as Usual;
- it is a useful process for developing the knowledge and skills of senior managers.
- Future developments

Building upon the information gained through all Business Excellence Reviews completed by the business to date, Counters has, in 1997, participated in a strategic benchmarking exercise. The study involved three separate trips, by over fifty managers (including forty of the most senior managers from across all the Post Office businesses). The benchmarking exercise concentrated upon the criteria from the Business Excellence Model which had been shown to have the greatest areas for improvement in successive reviews. Four companies took part in the study: BT, Hewlett Packard, Rank Xerox and Nortel. The companies were chosen because they were known to be high performers in the criteria being benchmarked. The information gleaned from this benchmarking study will be used to inform Counters' continuing use of the Business Excellence Model at all levels within the business.

For further information, please contact:

Ralph Milne,
Business Excellence Deployment Manager
Northern House
7 King Street
Leeds LS1 2HH
Tel: 0113 237 2708

Business excellence in a European Award winner - Design to Distribution Ltd

Company profile

Design to Distribution Limited, D2D, are a part of the Celestica Group of companies, but was previously an ICL subsidiary.

Based in the UK, they make and assemble printed circuit boards (PCBs), which they distribute world-wide, and support by after-sales services and through repair and refurbishment. In addition, they manufacture products ranging from personal computers and UNIX workstations to mainframes, retail point of sale terminals and scanners on behalf of customers.

D2D are based in the following main sites:

- Kidsgrove, Staffordshire (1800 people)
- Ashton-under-Lyne, Manchester (300)
- Bradwell Wood, Staffordshire (300)
- Byley, Cheshire (100)

In the electronics manufacturing services market place, Celestica is ranked number three with revenues of over £2.5 billion in 1996.

Self assessment

In 1983, following potentially serious financial difficulties, ICL embarked on a process of radical change that fundamentally altered their culture and attitude towards customers. In short, they became far more market-driven.

Crucial to the new philosophy was a commitment to quality, heavily influenced by the formidable competition the UK faced at that time from the Far East, particularly Japan. Dayvon Goodsell, D2D's quality manager, was responsible for taking ICL's corporate quality programmes and tailoring them for the manufacturing operation. Many of his early initiatives were based on re-examining processes which, in a manufacturing company, made sense. For example, the company adopted the Philip Crosby methodologies. D2D became one of the first organisations to be accredited with the ISO 9002 quality registration in 1988, and, in 1989, their Ashton-under-Lyne plant won 'Management Today' magazine's Best Factory competition. They had also just received the British Quality Award. However, although they were by now recognised as pioneers, competitive benchmarking showed that they still needed to improve their performance. Managers had become obsessed with the process by which things were accomplished, while forgetting the purpose or end goal.

D2D went back to the drawing board and began working with the European Foundation for Quality Management and the EFQM/BQF model. The company believed that the EFQM had devised a Quality Business Model, which used what was good in the Baldrige Award, while encouraging companies to take a more all-round approach. The model demonstrated that quality is not an end in itself - a popular misconception that has led to much scepticism about its value.

Initially, in 1991, self assessment was originated using the Malcolm Baldrige model, but as the EQA model gained credibility, in 1991/92 the company changed to the EFQM/BQF Model. Early self assessments used electronic meeting aids, such as the proprietary 'Option Finder' to assist initial analysis and to explain the model and its purpose.

D2D now have approximately 70 managers trained as UK/EQA assessors and able to apply this process. Teams collect data and views in a 'proforma template format' against each criterion or criterion part. Teams pulled from the pool of trained assessors make judgement. Recent learning has shown that views on 'deployment' often vary significantly, and structured questionnaire approaches have been introduced to test views at all levels, on key issues,

In 1993 an award application was made with the result that the company won a European Quality Award prize. In 1994 a further application was made, and this time they were nominated outright winners of The European Quality Award. Extracts from this award winning application are given in the next section of this chapter.

The benefits being obtained

At D2D, quality and self assessment is not a religion. It is seen as a competitive differentiator for the business but also as something that must provide value for money. Since the early 1980's, staff productivity has improved by over 300 per cent and the company has reduced quality losses, or costs of non-conformance, by an average of £2 to £3 million per annum.
The use of the EFQM/BQF Model for self assessment and as a strategic business planning tool has provided the drive to achieve this 'better all-round' approach to quality and now forms the backbone to D2D's philosophy for continuous improvement.

Future Developments

D2D believe they have a successful and stable self assessment process. Self assessment will continue as an ongoing process to help drive business planning.

For further information contact:

Dayvon Goodsell
D2D Ltd
West Avenue
Kidsgrove
Stoke on Trent
ST7 1TL

Summary

This chapter illustrates what some organisations have achieved with Business Excellence, and should serve as strong motivation for those organisations just starting out on the Business Excellence journey. On this aspirational note, the main body of the book is complete.

In the three appendices that follow, there is further material to support assessments:-

Appendix One contains a detailed description of how to score an organisation against the Improved Model, using the RADAR card.

Appendix Two contains a complete set of proformas to enable the reader to gather data, in a systematic way, as a precursor to taking part in an assessment.

Appendix Three contains contact details for key organisations working in Business Excellence, and provides brief details of some of the BQC range of publications referred to in this book.

Appendix One Use of scoring mechanisms

1.1 Why is scoring important?

For most people involved in self assessment, the main aim of the exercise is the identification and use of a list of organisational strengths and, perhaps more importantly, areas for improvement. They believe that by doing this, and then using the information to compose action plans, they will be able to drive the organisation forward. So why is scoring so important in this context?

Our experience has shown that management teams can easily agree the strengths and areas for improvement in their own part of an organisation. However, if they are then asked to give a score to reflect their perception of the organisation's achievement as a whole, responses reveal wide variations.

This means that, even though there has been agreement on the issues, there are significant differences of opinion about either their relative importance or the pervasiveness of the strengths or areas for improvement. In such circumstances, there can clearly be no satisfactory agreement about the way forward or, indeed how much effort is required to effect improvement.

In this situation the use of a scoring technique can provide a means whereby teams can:

- understand the current position of the organisation;
- evaluate the need for and impact of change;
- begin to control 'out-of-control' situations;
- ensure that gains achieved are maintained and maximised throughout the organisation;
- set priorities and schedules for improvement;
- focus on the rate of change and its improvement;
- make comparisons with others both within and outside the organisation;
- identify new customer requirements, the need for training, etc....

However there are 'dangers' inherent in using a scoring process such as:

- focusing too closely on the score rather than the learning form the self assessment;
- concentrating on the recognition aspects of using a model and self assessment and losing objectivity;
- over activity for short term improvement and results including the easy improvement initiatives at the expense of the really important issues;
- setting too many objectives to improve too many areas when closer prioritisation would deliver 'more for less'.

Thus, it must be remembered that the purpose of scoring is not just to give an organisation an overall mark for performance for comparative purposes. It will also enable the management team to compare their assessment with that of their colleagues and then to come to a consensus that positions the organisation's current level of achievement as they see it as a group.

1.2 Background to all scoring methods

So, to enhance the credibility of the application of self assessment, it is necessary to ensure that scoring is consistent. This is vital in generating confidence and in determining whether or not an organisation has moved forward.

The problem is that 'scoring' based on the UKQA/EQA process is not an exact science and does require a heavy element of judgement. It is not the simple application of a checklist with 'yes' or 'no' answers. When scoring an organisation, trained assessors are expected to be able to conform to a band of around plus or minus 70 points out of a total potential score of 1,000 points. Although this book is not intended to provide the means for readers to become fully trained assessors, it is useful to be generally familiar with the scoring process in order to glean a greater knowledge of the models and of the criteria on which they are based.

In parallel with the launch of the improved Model in 1999, the EFQM also introduced the RADAR concept of scoring. RADAR stands for **R**esults, **A**pproach, **D**eployment **A**ssessment and **R**eview.

The principle is that an organisation needs to:
* Be clear about the results it is to achieve to successfully meet the expectations of its stakeholders
* Put approaches in place that will drive towards those results
* Ensure the approaches are extensively implemented in a structured way
* Determine how effective are both its approaches and their deployment and implement improvements to continue the drive towards the desired results

In understanding the elements of scoring the first factor to be established is that for both 'enabler criteria' and 'results criteria' the scoring structure is multi-dimensional. For instance when scoring enablers, assessors are looking at the performance in three dimensions, namely the 'nature of the approach', the 'degree of deployment' that has been achieved and the 'assessment and review' to determine effectiveness and improve.

Similarly, when looking at a results criterion assessors are looking at both the 'excellence of the actual results achieved', and at the 'scope, or breadth of coverage of the results' presented. Success in these areas is judged against certain assessment themes.

Looking first at the factors used when determining a score for enablers. Diagram 14a lists the elements that assessors would be looking for in determining the appropriateness of the approaches and the extent they are used within the organisation.

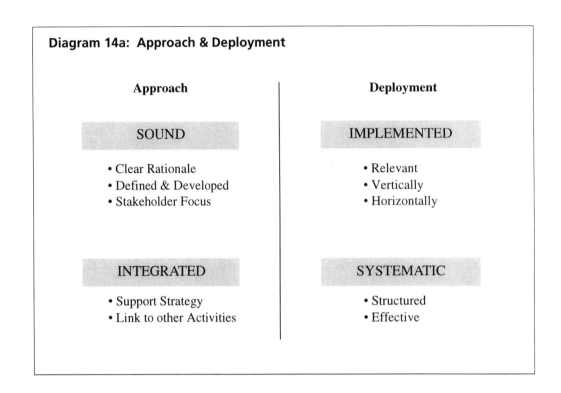

Diagram 14a: Approach & Deployment

Approach

SOUND

• Clear Rationale
• Defined & Developed
• Stakeholder Focus

INTEGRATED

• Support Strategy
• Link to other Activities

Deployment

IMPLEMENTED

• Relevant
• Vertically
• Horizontally

SYSTEMATIC

• Structured
• Effective

Diagram 14b shows the third dimension that assessors use to determine how effective is both the approach and deployment.

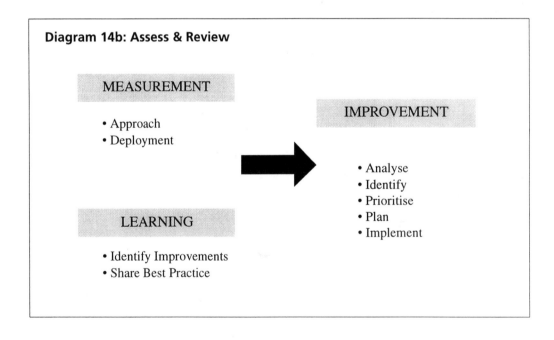

Diagram 14b: Assess & Review

MEASUREMENT

• Approach
• Deployment

LEARNING

• Identify Improvements
• Share Best Practice

IMPROVEMENT

• Analyse
• Identify
• Prioritise
• Plan
• Implement

They are looking for an organisation review to ascertain or confirm that the original purpose of the approach is actually being achieved in a business effective manner. They want to know if improvements designed to achieve a better approach have been determined, and if those improvements have been, and are being, implemented.

For the results criteria, Diagram 15 lists the requirements that would be considered when determining a score, using both the 'performance achieved' and the 'scope' dimensions of the results. With the help of additional information contained within the RADAR scoring matrices assessors are able to score each of the dimensions of an enabler or results criterion, and obtain an overall score.

Diagram 15: Results

Results	Scope
Positive Trends	Relevant
Sustained Performance	Some
Internal Targets	Many
External Comparisons	Most
Caused by Approach	All
Best in Class	

When undertaking self assessment, organisations may wish to consider, initially, either not scoring at all, or using very simplified scoring mechanisms. However, it is worth remembering that by using the RADAR 'calibrated' scoring mechanism the organisation has the benefit of being able to compare its scoring profile with that of organisations which enter for these awards. Section 1.3, provides details of the RADAR scoring metric. Section 1.4 provides a simpler, but calibrated metric, for 'beginners'. Section 1.5 provides comparative scoring data from EQA applicants.

1.3 Using the RADAR scoring matrices

The RADAR scoring matrices, provided separately with this book, contain the full scoring metrics. Chart 1 should be applied for each Enabler sub-criterion and Chart 2 for each Result sub-criterion. UKQA/EQA assessors are trained for three days on these mechanisms, before becoming appropriately qualified.

When using this process, a percentage score should be assigned for each criterion or sub-criterion section and transferred to the points scoring summary sheet to record individual criterion percentages. These are then converted to overall or average percentages and to weighted 'award points' (see page 77). An analysis of strengths and areas for improvement for each sub-criterion should be completed before using the scoring matrices.

The advice given to assessors when they are determining an organisation's performance against a criterion is to score each of the elements separately considering each of the attributes in turn. The boxes on the matrix give a visual display of the judgement being formed.

But how do you combine the score of the different elements? The normal approach is to start by taking the arithmetic average of the percentage score given for each of the elements. However, this can lead to some skewed results particularly when there are significant differences across the scores for the different elements. This is even more the case when one of the scores for a dimension is close to zero. An approach has therefore been refined over the years, which starts by taking an arithmetic average. The assessor should then consider whether this properly reflects the organisation's performance on a linear scale from zero (this organisation has achieved nothing) to a 100% score (this organisation is as good as one could reasonably expect in today's situation and is a role model). The assessor then applies his/her management judgement to adjust the score up or down. In this context, note that 50% is not an 'average' score. Award winning organisation's total scores are typically only 750 points, or less, out of 1000 possible.

Points Scoring Summary using RADAR Score Cards

1 Enablers Criteria

Criterion Number	1	%	2	%	3	%	4	%	5	%
Sub-Criterion	1a		2a		3a		4a		5a	
Sub-Criterion	1b		2b		3b		4b		5b	
Sub-Criterion	1c		2c		3c		4c		5c	
Sub-Criterion	1d		2d		3d		4d		5d	
Sub-Criterion			2e		3e		4e		5e	
Sum of Sub-criteria										
	÷4		÷5		÷5		÷5		÷5	
Criterion Score awarded										

Note: The criterion score awarded is the arithmetic average of the overall % scores of the sub-criteria

2 Results Criteria

Criterion Number	6	%		7	%		8	%		9	%	
Sub-Criterion	6a		x0.75	7a		x0.75	8a		x0.25	9a		x0.50
Sub-Criterion	6b		x0.25	7b		x0.25	8b		x0.75	9b		x0.50
Criterion Score awarded												

Note: The criterion score awarded is the total (a+b) of the weighted overall % scores.

3 Calculation of Total Points

Criterion	Score Awarded	factor	Points Awarded
1 Leadership		x 1.0	
2 Policy & Strategy		x 0.8	
3 People		x 0.9	
4 Partnerships & Resources		x 0.9	
5 Processes		x 1.4	
6 Customer Results		x 2.0	
7 People Results		x 0.9	
8 Society Results		x 0.6	
9 Key Performance Results		x 1.5	
Total Points Awarded			

-   *Enter the score awarded to each sub-criterion sections 1 and 2 above) to obtain the overall criterion score.*

-   *Multiply each criterion score by the appropriate factor to give points awarded (section 3).*

-   *Add points awarded to each criterion to give total points awarded for application.*

1.4 Using 'snapshot' scoring charts

Readers using the self assessment process for the first time may be prepared to sacrifice a degree of scoring 'purity' and accuracy in exchange for a simpler and potentially more easily applied scoring system. The 'snapshot score charts' coupled with their scoring summary sheet provide just such a method.

To use this method readers should first complete an analysis of strengths and areas for improvement for each criterion or sub-criterion (see Appendix 2) and then make the 'scoring decisions' illustrated on the snapshot charts. In other words readers should list their decision1, 2 and 3 scores, total scores, and multiply by a factor of 2 for enablers or 2.5 for results criteria, to obtain an approximate UKQA/EQA percentage score. This process is perhaps most useful for quick initial assessments and is typically not regarded as an 'ultimate' solution.

'Snapshot' Scorecard: Chart 1. Enablers

Decision 1. Score Approaches				
Doing Nothing	Just Starting	Some relevant, soundly based approaches in place	Many proven relevant well integrated approaches	Role model approaches fully integrated into normal working practices

Score	0	4	8	12	16

Decision 2. Score Deployment				
Not Started	Integrated into less than 25% of full potential	Integrated into less than 50% of full potential	Integrated into less than 75% of full potential	Deployed to full potential

Score	0	4	8	12	16

Decision 3. Score Evaluation Processes				
Non-existent	Occasional	Some evidence of review and refinement	Regular reviews and evidence of change/ improvement	All approaches regularly reviewed and improvements implemented

Score	0	4	8	12	16

Criteria	Decision 1 Score	Decision 2 Score	Decision 3 Score	Total Score (1+2+3)	X Factor	Predicted Overall %
1a					2.0	
1b					2.0	
1c					2.0	
1d					2.0	
2a					2.0	
2b					2.0	
2c					2.0	
2d					2.0	
2e					2.0	
3a					2.0	
3b					2.0	
3c					2.0	
3d					2.0	
3e					2.0	
4a					2.0	
4b					2.0	
4c					2.0	
4d					2.0	
4e					2.0	
5a					2.0	
5b					2.0	
5c					2.0	
5d					2.0	
5e					2.0	

Transfer predicted overall % scores to Points Scoring Summary Overleaf

'Snapshot' Scorecard: Chart 2. The Results

Decision 1. Scope of Measurement				
No relevant measurements	Few relevant measurements	Some to many measurements of relevant parameters	Regular measurement of most relevant parameters	Regular measurement of all relevant parameters
Score 0	4	8	12	16

Note: Relevant means proven to be of value to the appropriate stakeholder(s)

Decision 2. Trends and Levels of Results				
On balance, overall negative trends exist	Some positive trends and satisfactory comparison with own targets	Positive trends over 3+ years and many favourable comparisons with own targets	Strongly positive trends over 3+ years and favourable comparisons with own targets in most areas	Strongly positive trends in all relevant results for 5+ years. Excellent comparisons against own targets
Score 0	4	8	12	16

Note: Trends should be demonstrable by readily available data sources

Decision 3. Analysis of Results				
No analysis	Analysis shows some results caused by approach. External comparisons not made	Some external comparisons made, where relevant. Some results caused by approach	Favourable comparisons with external organisations in many relevant areas	Excellent comparisons with competitors and/or best in class organisations
Score 0	1	2	4	8

Criteria	Decision 1 Score	Decision 2 Score	Decision 3 Score	Total Score (1+2+3)	X Factor	Predicted Overall %
6a					2.5	
6b					2.5	
7a					2.5	
7b					2.5	
8a					2.5	
8b					2.5	
9a					2.5	
9b					2.5	

Transfer predicted overall % scores to Points Scoring Summary Overleaf

Points Scoring Summary using 'Snapshot' Score Cards

1 Enablers Criteria

Criterion Number	1	%	2	%	3	%	4	%	5	%
Sub-Criterion	1a		2a		3a		4a		5a	
Sub-Criterion	1b		2b		3b		4b		5b	
Sub-Criterion	1c		2c		3c		4c		5c	
Sub-Criterion	1d		2d		3d		4d		5d	
Sub-Criterion			2e		3e		4e		5e	
Sum of Sub-criteria										
	÷4		÷5		÷5		÷5		÷5	
Criterion Score awarded										

Note: The criterion score awarded is the arithmetic average of the overall % scores of the sub-criteria

2 Results Criteria

Criterion Number	6	%			7	%			8	%			9	%		
Sub-Criterion	6a		x0.75		7a		x0.75		8a		x0.25		9a		x0.50	
Sub-Criterion	6b		x0.25		7b		x0.25		8b		x0.75		9b		x0.50	
Criterion Score awarded																

Note: The criterion score awarded is the total (a+b) of the weighted overall % scores.

3 Calculation of Total Points

Criterion	Score Awarded	factor	Points Awarded
1 Leadership		x 1.0	
2 Policy & Strategy		x 0.8	
3 People		x 0.9	
4 Partnerships & Resources		x 0.9	
5 Processes		x 1.4	
6 Customer Results		x 2.0	
7 People Results		x 0.9	
8 Society Results		x 0.6	
9 Key Performance Results		x 1.5	
Total Points Awarded			

- *Enter the score awarded to each sub-criterion sections 1 and 2 above) to obtain the overall criterion score.*
- *Multiply each criterion score by the appropriate factor to give points awarded (section 3).*
- *Add points awarded to each criterion to give total points awarded for application.*

1.5 Comparing your scores

One advantage of applying the EFQM/BQF calibrated scoring mechanism is that it enables organisations to compare their scores with these organisations applying for the European Award. These are presented as cumulative data, covering the scores of all applicants since the Award was established in 1992, up to and including 1998.

Distribution of Scores for all applicants 1992-98

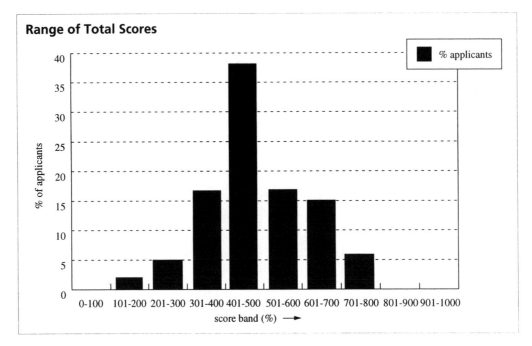

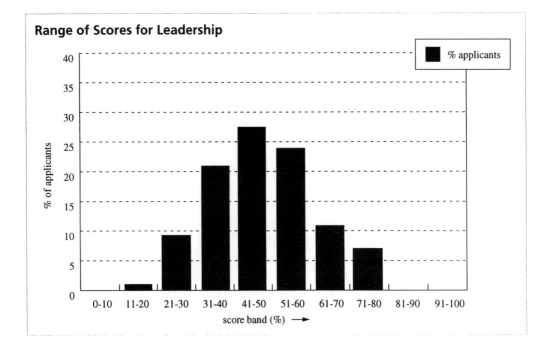

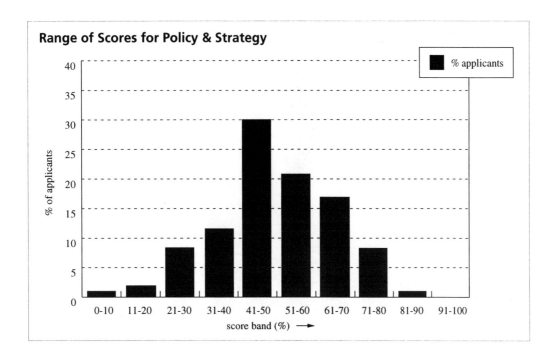

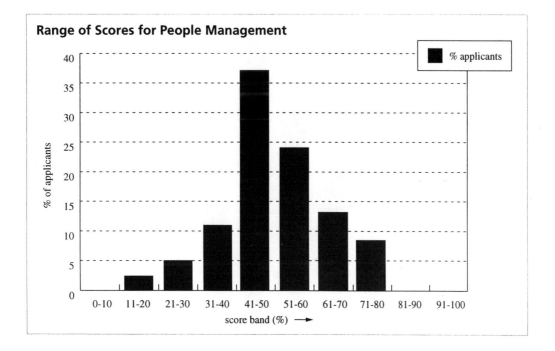

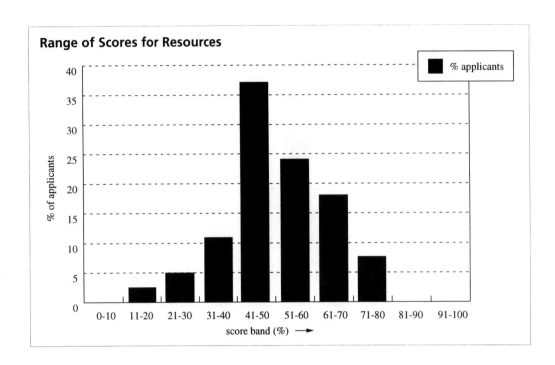

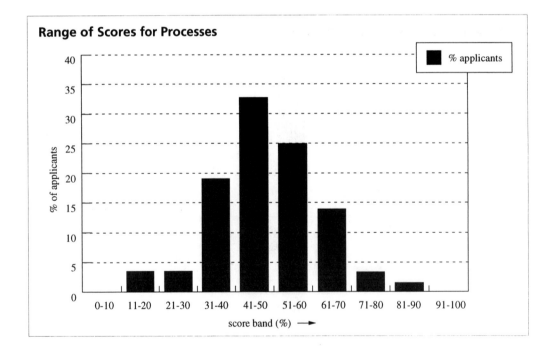

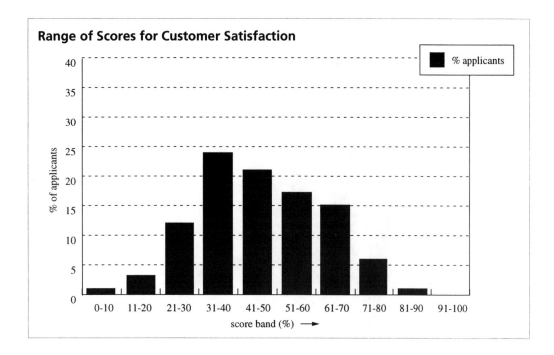

Range of Scores for Customer Satisfaction

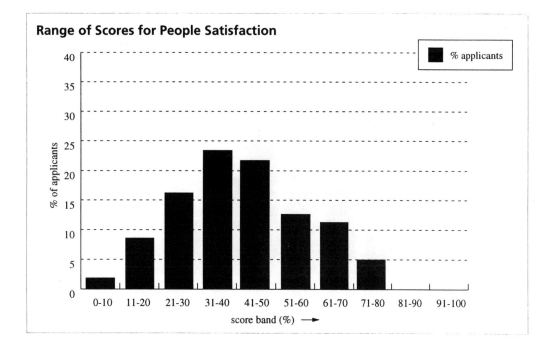

Range of Scores for People Satisfaction

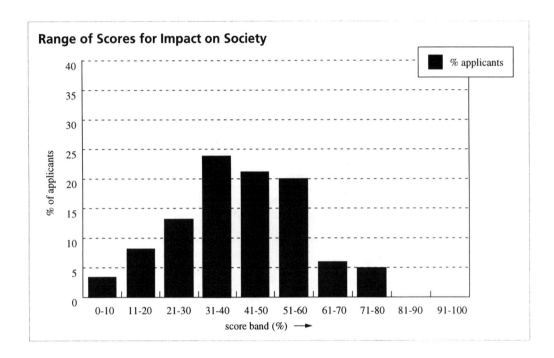

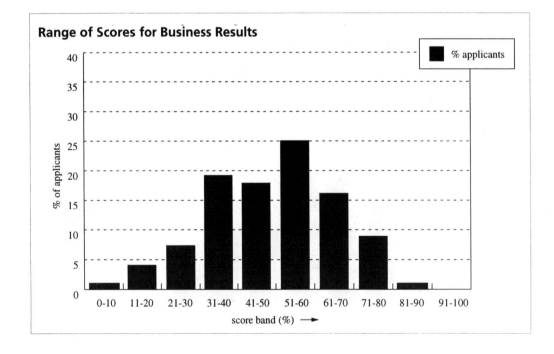

This tells us that the 'average' applicant for the European Award has a scoring profile:-

Leadership	48%	Customer Satisfaction	46%	
Policy & Strategy	50%	People Satisfaction	42%	*Giving an average*
People Management	50%	Impact on Society	41%	*score of 477 points*
Resources	52%	Business Results	49%	
Processes	49%			

Appendix Two: A Resource Kit

Undertaking a workshop assessment is an ideal way to gain management commitment to using the Model, increasing their understanding of it and putting a first 'stake in the ground'. If you want an assessment that is based on more than just the perceptions of the management team then more structured data gathering is required. A simple solution is to use a set of proformas which can guide the data gathering. This section includes a tried and tested proforma format developed with our client base and now updated to align with the 1999 improved Model.

At the beginning of each criterion there is a diagramatic version of it showing the various inter-relationships. There is then a proforma for each sub criterion which leads the user step-by-step through the process of data gathering to ultimately developing a balanced view of strengths and areas for improvement.

1: Leadership

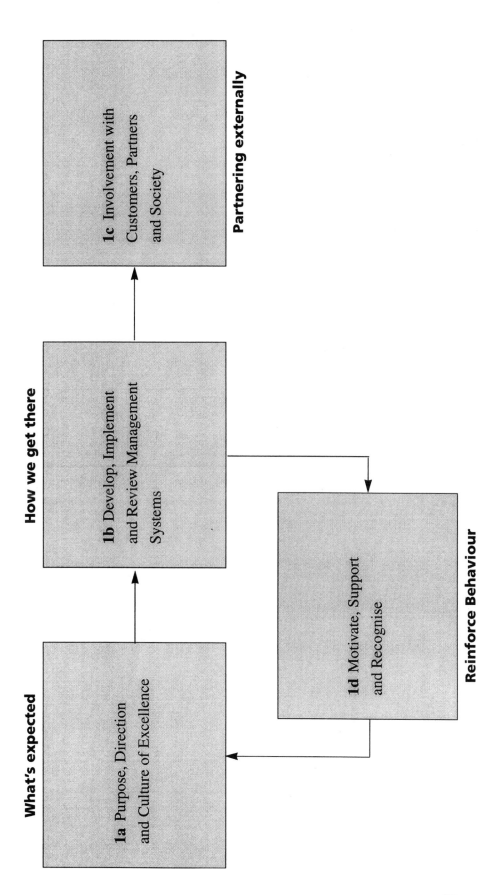

What's expected

1a Purpose, Direction and Culture of Excellence

How we get there

1b Develop, Implement and Review Management Systems

Partnering externally

1c Involvement with Customers, Partners and Society

Reinforce Behaviour

1d Motivate, Support and Recognise

How leaders develop and facilitate the achievement of the mission and vision, develop values required for long term success and implement these via appropriate actions and behaviours, and are personally involved in ensuring that the organisation's management system is developed and implemented.

1a Leaders develop the mission, vision and values and are role models of a culture of Excellence.

This may include:

How are leaders involved in establishing the mission, vision and the behaviours expected in the organisation?

Does the actual behaviour of leaders reinforce the values, behaviour and expectations set by the organisation?

Do they personally get involved in improvement activities? Is this involvement visible outside their department?

How do they gather feedback to review their leadership style and use it to improve? (e.g. through 360 degree appraisal)

Are leaders involved and visible in activities such as goal-setting, prioritising improvements, and reviewing improvement performance?

How do leaders plan to stimulate innovation and creativity and empower their people?

How do leaders focus on the importance of learning?

How do leaders emphasise the importance of co-operation across the organisation?

Leadership 1a

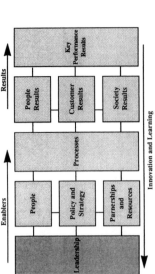

Enablers — Results

Innovation and Learning

The EFQM Excellence Model is a registered Trademark

Step 1. Assess importance of criterion

	These are not key issues	These issues are moderately important	These issues are important	These issues are critical
	(0)	(1)	(2)	(3)
Importance Rating				

Note: Tick a box to indicate your view of the importance of this criterion (note, the description of the criterion is the words after 1a)

Steps 2-5. Activity/Behaviour list

2. Activity /Behaviour	3. Duration of use	4. Deployment	5. How reviewed?

Step 2. List specific existing activities, policies, processes, behaviours and practices that impact on this criterion

Step 3. For each activity listed in step 2, list how long you have been using each policy, process or practice (years/months)

Step 4. List to what extent you want to deploy each policy, process and practice and how far they have been deployed to date

    (eg by site, organisational level, department, activity, product etc)

Step 5. List how and how often you review the effectiveness of each activity and the overall process

Note: Annotate your comments onto the activity/behaviour list above

Step 6. List improvements resulting from reviews

Step 7. Review your comments on steps 1 to 6 as a whole, and form and record an opinion on the success of the **approaches** used, their **deployment** and the **review** of them. List this as a set of composite perceived strengths and areas for improvement. The scoring cards should be used to help your thoughts. The scoring card indicates which aspects of approach, deployment and review should influence your score.

Perceived strengths (+)

Perceived areas for improvement (-)

Note: List also areas for improvement relevant activities that you feel should be initiated and are not at present undertaken

Approach	%
Deployment	%
Assess & Review	%
Overall	%

How leaders develop and facilitate the achievement of the mission and vision, develop values required for long term success and implement these via appropriate actions and behaviours, and are personally involved in ensuring that the organisation's management system is developed and implemented.

Leadership 1b

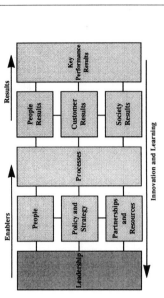

Enablers | Results

Innovation and Learning

The EFQM Excellence Model is a registered Trademark

1b Leaders are personally involved in ensuring the organisation's management system is developed, implemented and continuously improved

This may include:

How is the organisation structured to deliver the strategy developed by its leaders?

How is process management systematically used?

How do leaders put in place a system for developing, implementing and updating the organisation's strategy?

How do leaders put in place a system for focusing on the key results indicating the success of the strategy?

How do leaders establish a process to implement their plan to stimulate innovation and creativity in their people?

Step 1. Assess importance of criterion

	These are not key issues	These issues are moderately important	These issues are important	These issues are critical
Importance Rating	(0)	(1)	(2)	(3)

Note: Tick a box to indicate your view of the importance of this criterion (note, the description of the criterion is the words after 1b)

Steps 2-5. Activity/Behaviour list

2. Activity /Behaviour	3. Duration of use	4. Deployment	5. How reviewed?

Step 2. List specific existing activities, policies, processes, behaviours and practices that impact on this criterion

Step 3. For each activity listed in step 2, list how long you have been using each policy, process or practice (years/months)

Step 4. List to what extent you want to deploy each policy, process and practice and how far they have been deployed to date
(eg by site, organisational level, department, activity, product etc)

Step 5. List how and how often you review the effectiveness of each activity and the overall process

Note: Annotate your comments onto the activity/behaviour list above

---

Step 6. List improvements resulting from reviews

Step 7. Review your comments on steps 1 to 6 as a whole, and form and record an opinion on the success of the **approaches** used, their **deployment** and the **review** of them. List this as a set of composite perceived strengths and areas for improvement. The scoring cards should be used to help your thoughts. The scoring card indicates which aspects of approach, deployment and review should influence your score.

Perceived strengths (+)	Perceived areas for improvement (-)

Note: List also areas for improvement relevant activities that you feel should be initiated and are not at present undertaken

Approach	%
Deployment	%
Assess & Review	%
Overall	%

How leaders develop and facilitate the achievement of the mission and vision, develop values required for long term success and implement these via appropriate actions and behaviours, and are personally involved in ensuring that the organisation's management system is developed and implemented.

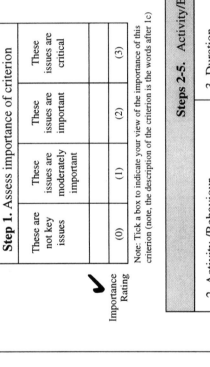

Leadership 1c

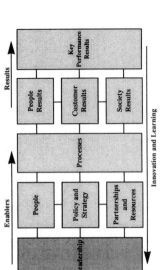

Enablers | Results

Innovation and Learning

The EFQM Excellence Model is a registered Trademark

1c Leaders are involved with customers, partners and representatives of society

This may include:

How do leaders prioritise their activities with different customer groups?

Do these contacts address joint improvement and partnership issues?

Are these contacts geared to identifying future needs before they become an issue (i.e. prevention based)?

Are leaders' memberships of professional bodies helpful in actively promoting Business Excellence?

Is recognition for excellence and continuous improvement provided outside the organisation, for example to customers, suppliers and other external stakeholders?

How are leaders directly involved in corporate citizenship activities?

How are leaders directly involved in developing partnerships with customers, suppliers and other external stakeholders?

Step 1. Assess importance of criterion

	These are not key issues	These issues are moderately important	These issues are important	These issues are critical
Importance Rating	(0)	(1)	(2)	(3)

Note: Tick a box to indicate your view of the importance of this criterion (note, the description of the criterion is the words after 1c)

Steps 2-5. Activity/Behaviour list

2. Activity /Behaviour	3. Duration of use	4. Deployment	5. How reviewed?

Step 2. List specific existing activities, policies, processes, behaviours and practices that impact on this criterion

Step 3. For each activity listed in step 2, list how long you have been using each policy, process or practice (years/months)

Step 4. List to what extent you want to deploy each policy, process and practice and how far they have been deployed to date

(eg by site, organisational level, department, activity, product etc)

Step 5. List how and how often you review the effectiveness of each activity and the overall process

Note: Annotate your comments onto the activity/behaviour list above

---

Step 6. List improvements resulting from reviews

Step 7. Review your comments on steps 1 to 6 as a whole, and form and record an opinion on the success of the **approaches** used, their **deployment** and the **review** of them. List this as a set of composite perceived strengths and areas for improvement. The scoring cards should be used to help your thoughts. The scoring card indicates which aspects of approach, deployment and review should influence your score.

Perceived strengths (+)	Perceived areas for improvement (-)

Note: List also areas for improvement relevant activities that you feel should be initiated and are not at present undertaken

Approach	%
Deployment	%
Assess & Review	%
Overall	%

How leaders develop and facilitate the achievement of the mission and vision, develop values required for long term success and implement these via appropriate actions and behaviours, and are personally involved in ensuring that the organisation's management system is developed and implemented.

Leadership 1d

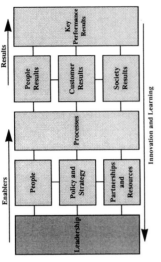

Enablers

Results

Innovation and Learning

The EFQM Excellence Model is a registered Trademark

1d Leaders motivate, support and recognise the organisation's people

This may include:

How do leaders deliberately make themselves accessible to their employees?

How do they communicate with their employees? Do they make specific opportunities to listen to them?

What processes exist to involve leaders in recognising individuals and teams for outstanding performance? How do leaders get involved personally with this recognition?

Is the performance of teams and individuals in excellence and continuous improvement recognised and rewarded at the same level as other business considerations, for example in comparison with any personal productivity objectives and bonus schemes?

What is the relative emphasis placed on team recognition versus individual recognition?

How do leaders clearly communicate where the organisation is going and how their people can contribute?

How do leaders support their people in making that contribution?

How do leaders emphasise the importance of improvement activity and make it possible for their people to get involved?

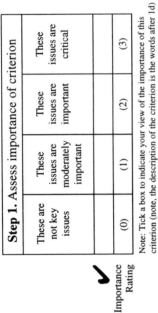

Step 1. Assess importance of criterion

	These are not key issues	These issues are moderately important	These issues are important	These issues are critical
Importance Rating	(0)	(1)	(2)	(3)

Note: Tick a box to indicate your view of the importance of this criterion (note, the description of the criterion is the words after 1d)

Steps 2-5. Activity/Behaviour list

2. Activity /Behaviour	3. Duration of use	4. Deployment	5. How reviewed?

Step 2. List specific existing activities, policies, processes, behaviours and practices that impact on this criterion

Step 3. For each activity listed in step 2, list how long you have been using each policy, process or practice (years/months)

Step 4. List to what extent you want to deploy each policy, process and practice and how far they have been deployed to date
(eg by site, organisational level, department, activity, product etc)

Step 5. List how and how often you review the effectiveness of each activity and the overall process

Note: Annotate your comments onto the activity/behaviour list above

Step 6. List improvements resulting from reviews

Step 7. Review your comments on steps 1 to 6 as a whole, and form and record an opinion on the success of the **approaches** used, their **deployment** and the **review** of them. List this as a set of composite perceived strengths and areas for improvement. The scoring cards should be used to help your thoughts. The scoring card indicates which aspects of approach, deployment and review should influence your score.

Perceived strengths (+)

Perceived areas for improvement (-)

Note: List also areas for improvement relevant activities that you feel should be initiated and are not at present undertaken

Approach	%
Deployment	%
Assess & Review	%
Overall	%

You have now completed Criterion 1 - Note any actions required

2: Policy & Strategy

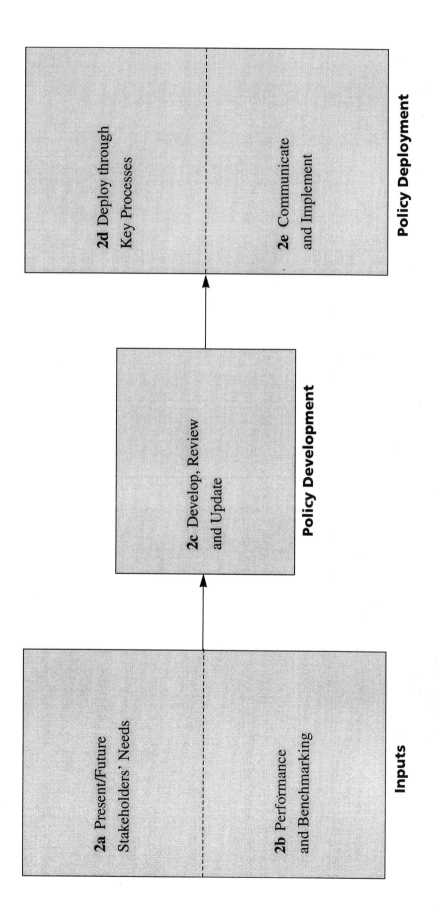

2a Present/Future Stakeholders' Needs

2b Performance and Benchmarking

Inputs

2c Develop, Review and Update

Policy Development

2d Deploy through Key Processes

2e Communicate and Implement

Policy Deployment

How the organisation implements its mission and vision via a clear stakeholder focused strategy, supported by relevant policies, plans, objectives, targets and processes

Policy and Strategy 2a

Enablers | Results

Leadership, People, Policy and Strategy, Partnerships and Resources, Processes, People Results, Customer Results, Society Results, Key Performance Results

Innovation and Learning

The EFQM Excellence Model is a registered Trademark

Step 1. Assess importance of criterion

	These are not key issues	These issues are moderately important	These issues are important	These issues are critical
Importance Rating	(0)	(1)	(2)	(3)

Note: Tick a box to indicate your view of the importance of this criterion (note, the description of the criterion is the words after 2a)

Steps 2-5. Activity/Behaviour list

2. Activity /Behaviour	3. Duration of use	4. Deployment	5. How reviewed?

2a Policy and Strategy are based on the present and future needs and expectations of stakeholders

This may include:

In developing business strategy, what use is made of results and data obtained as:

• feedback from staff
• feedback from customers
• feedback from suppliers
• feedback from other partners

How are the needs of other stakeholders taken into account? e.g. society, shareholders, etc

How is a current and forward view of the market place determined?

Is the information used at a strategic level rather than only for tactical issues?

Step 2. List specific existing activities, policies, processes, behaviours and practices that impact on this criterion

Step 3. For each activity listed in step 2, list how long you have been using each policy, process or practice (years/months)

Step 4. List to what extent you want to deploy each policy, process and practice and how far they have been deployed to date (eg by site, organisational level, department, activity, product etc)

Step 5. List how and how often you review the effectiveness of each activity and the overall process

Note: Annotate your comments onto the activity/behaviour list above

Step 6. List improvements resulting from reviews

Step 7. Review your comments on steps 1 to 6 as a whole, and form and record an opinion on the success of the **approaches** used, their **deployment** and the **review** of them. List this as a set of composite perceived strengths and areas for improvement. The scoring cards should be used to help your thoughts. The scoring card indicates which aspects of approach, deployment and review should influence your score.

Perceived strengths (+)	Perceived areas for improvement (-)

Note: List also areas for improvement relevant activities that you feel should be initiated and are not at present undertaken

Approach	%
Deployment	%
Assess & Review	%
Overall	%

How the organisation implements its mission and vision via a clear stakeholder focused strategy, supported by relevant policies, plans, objectives, targets and processes

The EFQM Excellence Model is a registered Trademark

2b Policy and Strategy are based on information from performance measurement, research, learning and creativity related activities

This may include:

In developing business strategy, what use is made of results and information obtained as:

- data on competitors
- data on new technologies
- data on legislative, socio-economic, environmental and regulatory issues

How are internal performance measures used to ensure strategies are realistic?

How are 'best in class' and other benchmarking data used to set stretch goals?

How is the result of organisational learning analysed to provide input to strategy?

Is all the information used at a strategic level rather than only for tactical issues?

Step 1. Assess importance of criterion			
These are not key issues	These issues are moderately important	These issues are important	These issues are critical
(0)	(1)	(2)	(3)

Importance Rating

Note: Tick a box to indicate your view of the importance of this criterion (note, the description of the criterion is the words after 2b)

Steps 2-5. Activity/Behaviour list

2. Activity /Behaviour	3. Duration of use	4. Deployment	5. How reviewed?

Step 2. List specific existing activities, policies, processes, behaviours and practices that impact on this criterion

Step 3. For each activity listed in step 2, list how long you have been using each policy, process or practice (years/months)

Step 4. List to what extent you want to deploy each policy, process and practice and how far they have been deployed to date

(eg by site, organisational level, department, activity, product etc)

Step 5. List how and how often you review the effectiveness of each activity and the overall process

Note: Annotate your comments onto the activity/behaviour list above

Step 6. List improvements resulting from reviews

Step 7. Review your comments on steps 1 to 6 as a whole, and form and record an opinion on the success of the **approaches** used, their **deployment** and the **review** of them. List this as a set of composite perceived strengths and areas for improvement. The scoring cards should be used to help your thoughts. The scoring card indicates which aspects of approach, deployment and review should influence your score.

Perceived strengths (+)

Perceived areas for improvement (-)

Approach	%
Deployment	%
Assess & Review	%
Overall	%

Note: List also areas for improvement relevant activities that you feel should be initiated and are not at present undertaken

How the organisation implements its mission and vision via a clear stakeholder focused strategy, supported by relevant policies, plans, objectives, targets and processes

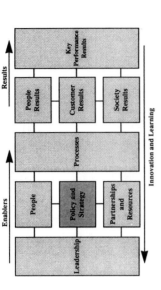

Enablers | Results

Leadership — People, Policy and Strategy, Partnerships and Resources — Processes — People Results, Customer Results, Society Results — Key Performance Results

Innovation and Learning

The EFQM Excellence Model is a registered Trademark

2c Policy and Strategy are developed, reviewed and updated

This may include:

How is the business strategy aligned with the mission, vision and values?

How does the organisation ensure a balance between the interests of its various stakeholders?

How does the organisation determine whether its strategy is broad enough to address all the issues relating to Business Excellence?

How is scenario planning used to manage risk?

How is the strategy linked to that of the organisation's partners?

How does the organisation focus on its critical success factors?

How is strategy reviewed to ensure it continues to be relevant and effective and then is updated when necessary?

How is the process of developing and updating strategy reviewed, as well as the content of the strategy itself?

Step 1. Assess importance of criterion

These are not key issues	These issues are moderately important	These issues are important	These issues are critical
(0)	(1)	(2)	(3)

Importance Rating

Note: Tick a box to indicate your view of the importance of this criterion (note, the description of the criterion is the words after 2c)

Steps 2-5. Activity/Behaviour list

2. Activity /Behaviour	3. Duration of use	4. Deployment	5. How reviewed?

Step 2. List specific existing activities, policies, processes, behaviours and practices that impact on this criterion

Step 3. For each activity listed in step 2, list how long you have been using each policy, process or practice (years/months)

Step 4. List to what extent you want to deploy each policy, process and practice and how far they have been deployed to date

(eg by site, organisational level, department, activity, product etc)

Step 5. List how and how often you review the effectiveness of each activity and the overall process

Note: Annotate your comments onto the activity/behaviour list above

---

Step 6. List improvements resulting from reviews

Step 7. Review your comments on steps 1 to 6 as a whole, and form and record an opinion on the success of the **approaches** used, their **deployment** and the **review** of them. List this as a set of composite perceived strengths and areas for improvement. The scoring cards should be used to help your thoughts. The scoring card indicates which aspects of approach, deployment and review should influence your score.

Perceived strengths (+)	Perceived areas for improvement (-)

Note: List also areas for improvement relevant activities that you feel should be initiated and are not at present undertaken

Approach	%
Deployment	%
Assess & Review	%
Overall	%

How the organisation implements its mission and vision via a clear stakeholder focused strategy, supported by relevant policies, plans, objectives, targets and processes

Policy and Strategy 2d

The EFQM Excellence Model is a registered Trademark

2d Policy and Strategy are deployed through a framework of key processes

This may include:

How has the organisation identified the end-to-end processes that are critical to its success?

How is their potential 'impact on the business' evaluated?

Have high level owners been appointed for the key processes?

How does the organisation regularly review the critical processes and key performance parameters that it needs to monitor, in order to achieve its objectives and deliver its strategy?

How are future stakeholder needs predicted and incorporated into the approach to critical process identification?

Step 1. Assess importance of criterion

	These are not key issues	These issues are moderately important	These issues are important	These issues are critical
Importance Rating	(0)	(1)	(2)	(3)

Note: Tick a box to indicate your view of the importance of this criterion (note, the description of the criterion is the words after 2d)

Steps 2-5. Activity/Behaviour list

2. Activity /Behaviour	3. Duration of use	4. Deployment	5. How reviewed?

Step 2. List specific existing activities, policies, processes, behaviours and practices that impact on this criterion

Step 3. For each activity listed in step 2, list how long you have been using each policy, process or practice (years/months)

Step 4. List to what extent you want to deploy each policy, process and practice and how far they have been deployed to date

(eg by site, organisational level, department, activity, product etc)

Step 5. List how and how often you review the effectiveness of each activity and the overall process

Note: Annotate your comments onto the activity/behaviour list above

---

Step 6. List improvements resulting from reviews

Step 7. Review your comments on steps 1 to 6 as a whole, and form and record an opinion on the success of the **approaches** used, their **deployment** and the **review** of them. List this as a set of composite perceived strengths and areas for improvement. The scoring cards should be used to help your thoughts. The scoring card indicates which aspects of approach, deployment and review should influence your score.

Perceived strengths (+)	Perceived areas for improvement (-)

Note: List also areas for improvement relevant activities that you feel should be initiated and are not at present undertaken

Approach	%
Deployment	%
Assess & Review	%
Overall	%

'How the organisation implements its mission and vision via a clear stakeholder focused strategy, supported by relevant policies, plans, objectives, targets and processes

2e Policy and Strategy are communicated and implemented

This may include:

How are annual plans aligned with the longer-term view?

How are communications on policy and strategy planned and prioritised?

Is the effectiveness of the communications evaluated and improved?

Does the organisation evaluate employees' awareness of the relevant aspects of policy and strategy?

How does strategy provide a framework for cascading targets and objectives?

The EFQM Excellence Model is a registered Trademark

Step 1. Assess importance of criterion

	These are not key issues	These issues are moderately important	These issues are important	These issues are critical
	(0)	(1)	(2)	(3)

Importance Rating

Note: Tick a box to indicate your view of the importance of this criterion (note, the description of the criterion is the words after 2e)

Steps 2-5. Activity/Behaviour list

2. Activity /Behaviour	3. Duration of use	4. Deployment	5. How reviewed?

Step 2. List specific existing activities, policies, processes, behaviours and practices that impact on this criterion

Step 3. For each activity listed in step 2, list how long you have been using each policy, process or practice (years/months)

Step 4. List to what extent you want to deploy each policy, process and practice and how far they have been deployed to date
(eg by site, organisational level, department, activity, product etc)

Step 5. List how and how often you review the effectiveness of each activity and the overall process

Note : Annotate your comments onto the activity/behaviour list above

Step 6. List improvements resulting from reviews

Step 7. Review your comments on steps 1 to 6 as a whole, and form and record an opinion on the success of the **approaches** used, their **deployment** and the **review** of them. List this as a set of composite perceived strengths and areas for improvement. The scoring cards should be used to help your thoughts. The scoring card indicates which aspects of approach, deployment and review should influence your score.

Perceived strengths (+)	Perceived areas for improvement (-)

Note: List also areas for improvement relevant activities that you feel should be initiated and are not at present undertaken

Approach	%
Deployment	%
Assess & Review	%
Overall	%

You have now completed Criterion 2 - Note any actions required

3: People

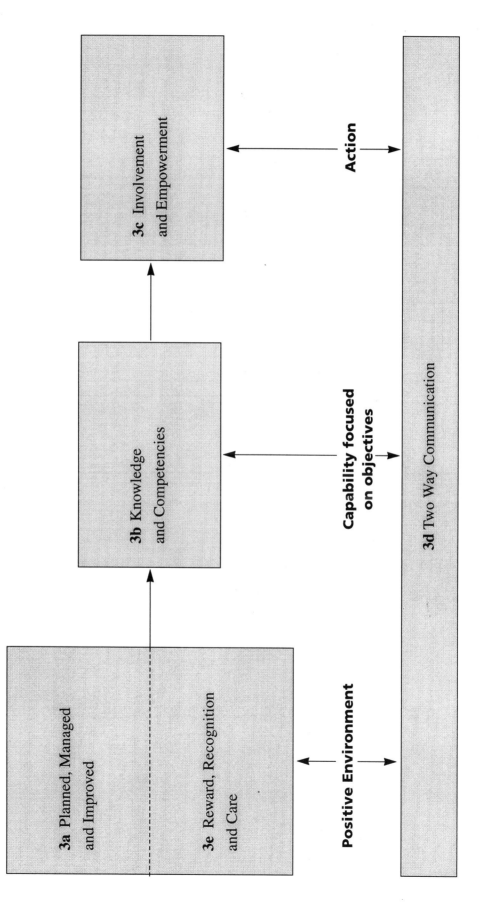

3a Planned, Managed and Improved

3e Reward, Recognition and Care

3b Knowledge and Competencies

3c Involvement and Empowerment

3d Two Way Communication

Positive Environment

Capability focused on objectives

Action

How the organisation manages, develops and releases the knowledge and full potential of its people at an individual, team-based and organisation-wide level, and plans these activities in order to support its policy and strategy and the effective operation of its processes

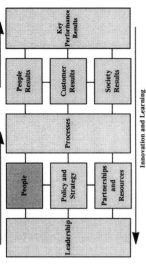

Enablers | Results

Leadership — People / Policy and Strategy / Partnerships and Resources — Processes — People Results / Customer Results / Society Results — Key Performance Results

Innovation and Learning

The EFQM Excellence Model is a registered Trademark

3a People resources are planned, managed and improved

This may include:

Are people plans (for example, hiring, training, development) aligned to the business plans and key processes?

Is there regular assessment of employee morale, and are the results made known and acted upon? eg. Updating policy and/or procedures

How do terms and conditions e.g. equal opportunities fit with stated policies on people as a stakeholder in the organisation?

Has the organisation revised working methods and structures by benchmarking external practices? (for example with self-directed work teams, flexible cells, etc)

How is career development planned?

Is there an effective recruitment policy/process in place to meet the organisations needs?

Have organisational structures been re-shaped to encourage innovation and creativity in process improvement?

Step 1. Assess importance of criterion

	These are not key issues	These issues are moderately important	These issues are important	These issues are critical	
Importance Rating	(0)	(1)	(2)	(3)	

Note: Tick a box to indicate your view of the importance of this criterion (note, the description of the criterion is the words after 3a)

Steps 2-5. Activity/Behaviour list

2. Activity /Behaviour	3. Duration of use	4. Deployment	5. How reviewed?

Step 2. List specific existing activities, policies, processes, behaviours and practices that impact on this criterion

Step 3. For each activity listed in step 2, list how long you have been using each policy, process or practice (years/months)

Step 4. List to what extent you want to deploy each policy, process and practice and how far they have been deployed to date

(eg by site, organisational level, department, activity, product etc)

Step 5. List how and how often you review the effectiveness of each activity and the overall process

Note: Annotate your comments onto the activity/behaviour list above

Step 6. List improvements resulting from reviews

Step 7. Review your comments on steps 1 to 6 as a whole, and form and record an opinion on the success of the **approaches** used, their **deployment** and the **review** of them. List this as a set of composite perceived strengths and areas for improvement. The scoring cards should be used to help your thoughts. The scoring card indicates which aspects of approach, deployment and review should influence your score.

Perceived strengths (+)

Perceived areas for improvement (-)

Note: List also areas for improvement relevant activities that you feel should be initiated and are not at present undertaken

Approach	%
Deployment	%
Assess & Review	%
Overall	%

How the organisation manages, develops and releases the knowledge and full potential of its people at an individual, team-based and organisation-wide level, and plans these activities in order to support its policy and strategy and the effective operation of its processes

People 3b

The EFQM Excellence Model is a registered Trademark

3b People's knowledge and competencies are identified, developed and sustained

This may include:

How are people's knowledge and competencies developed to meet the current and future needs of the organisation?

How is learning actively encouraged at individual, team and organisational level?

How is work experience, secondments or job rotation used to develop staff?

How are individual and team objectives aligned with that of the organisation strategy?

Are people's skills developed by working in teams?

How are targets / objectives regularly reviewed?

How are targets and objectives updated if necessary?

How is individual or team performance against objectives assessed?

How are individuals given help if their performance is falling short?

Step 1. Assess importance of criterion

	These are not key issues	These issues are moderately important	These issues are important	These issues are critical
Importance Rating	(0)	(1)	(2)	(3)

Note: Tick a box to indicate your view of the importance of this criterion (note, the description of the criterion is the words after 3b)

Steps 2-5. Activity/Behaviour list

2. Activity /Behaviour	3. Duration of use	4. Deployment	5. How reviewed?

114

Step 2. List specific existing activities, policies, processes, behaviours and practices that impact on this criterion

Step 3. For each activity listed in step 2, list how long you have been using each policy, process or practice (years/months)

Step 4. List to what extent you want to deploy each policy, process and practice and how far they have been deployed to date

(eg by site, organisational level, department, activity, product etc)

Step 5. List how and how often you review the effectiveness of each activity and the overall process

Note: Annotate your comments onto the activity/behaviour list above

---

Step 6. List improvements resulting from reviews

Step 7. Review your comments on steps 1 to 6 as a whole, and form and record an opinion on the success of the **approaches** used, their **deployment** and the **review** of them. List this as a set of composite perceived strengths and areas for improvement. The scoring cards should be used to help your thoughts. The scoring card indicates which aspects of approach, deployment and review should influence your score.

Perceived strengths (+)	Perceived areas for improvement (-)

Note: List also areas for improvement relevant activities that you feel should be initiated and are not at present undertaken

Approach	%
Deployment	%
Assess & Review	%
Overall	%

How the organisation manages, develops and releases the knowledge and full potential of its people at an individual, team-based and organisation-wide level, and plans these activities in order to support its policy and strategy and the effective operation of its processes

People 3c

3c People are involved and empowered

This may include:

What approaches are in place to not only encourage involvement but stimulate innovation and creativity?

How are individuals given the opportunity to contribute to continuous improvement?

How are teams given the opportunity to contribute to continuous improvement ? (both line and cross-functional teams)

Are people empowered to make changes within their own area without upwards referral?

Enablers | Results

Leadership · People · Policy and Strategy · Partnerships and Resources · Processes · People Results · Customer Results · Society Results · Key Performance Results

Innovation and Learning

The EFQM Excellence Model is a registered Trademark

Step 1. Assess importance of criterion

	These are not key issues	These issues are moderately important	These issues are important	These issues are critical
Importance Rating	(0)	(1)	(2)	(3)

Note: Tick a box to indicate your view of the importance of this criterion (note, the description of the criterion is the words after 3c)

Steps 2-5. Activity/Behaviour list

2. Activity /Behaviour	3. Duration of use	4. Deployment	5. How reviewed?

Step 2. List specific existing activities, policies, processes, behaviours and practices that impact on this criterion

Step 3. For each activity listed in step 2, list how long you have been using each policy, process or practice (years/months)

Step 4. List to what extent you want to deploy each policy, process and practice and how far they have been deployed to date
(eg by site, organisational level, department, activity, product etc)

Step 5. List how and how often you review the effectiveness of each activity and the overall process

Note: Annotate your comments onto the activity/behaviour list above

Step 6. List improvements resulting from reviews

Step 7. Review your comments on steps 1 to 6 as a whole, and form and record an opinion on the success of the **approaches** used, their **deployment** and the **review** of them. List this as a set of composite perceived strengths and areas for improvement. The scoring cards should be used to help your thoughts. The scoring card indicates which aspects of approach, deployment and review should influence your score.

Perceived strengths (+)	Perceived areas for improvement (-)

Note: List also areas for improvement relevant activities that you feel should be initiated and are not at present undertaken

Approach	%
Deployment	%
Assess & Review	%
Overall	%

How the organisation manages, develops and releases the knowledge and full potential of its people at an individual, team-based and organisation-wide level, and plans these activities in order to support its policy and strategy and the effective operation of its processes

3d People and the organisation have a dialogue

This may include:

Have the communications needs of employees been identified?

Have the formal company approaches been assessed against these needs and modified/ supplemented as applicable?

How does the organisation evaluate the level of understanding of the message communicated?

How systematic is the sharing of knowledge and best practice both from within and external to the organisation?

How is two-way communication encouraged?

What emphasis is given to cross-functional communication?

What steps are taken to continuously improve top-down, bottom-up and cross-functional communications?

The EFQM Excellence Model is a registered Trademark

Step 1. Assess importance of criterion

	These are not key issues	These issues are moderately important	These issues are important	These issues are critical
Importance Rating	(0)	(1)	(2)	(3)

Note: Tick a box to indicate your view of the importance of this criterion (note, the description of the criterion is the words after 3d)

Steps 2-5. Activity/Behaviour list

2. Activity /Behaviour	3. Duration of use	4. Deployment	5. How reviewed?

Step 2. List specific existing activities, policies, processes, behaviours and practices that impact on this criterion

Step 3. For each activity listed in step 2, list how long you have been using each policy, process or practice (years/months)

Step 4. List to what extent you want to deploy each policy, process and practice and how far they have been deployed to date (eg by site, organisational level, department, activity, product etc)

Step 5. List how and how often you review the effectiveness of each activity and the overall process

Note: Annotate your comments onto the activity/behaviour list above

Step 6. List improvements resulting from reviews

Step 7. Review your comments on steps 1 to 6 as a whole, and form and record an opinion on the success of the **approaches** used, their **deployment** and the **review** of them. List this as a set of composite perceived strengths and areas for improvement. The scoring cards should be used to help your thoughts. The scoring card indicates which aspects of approach, deployment and review should influence your score.

Perceived strengths (+)	Perceived areas for improvement (-)

Note: List also areas for improvement relevant activities that you feel should be initiated and are not at present undertaken

Approach	%
Deployment	%
Assess & Review	%
Overall	%

How the organisation manages, develops and releases the knowledge and full potential of its people at an individual, team-based and organisation-wide level, and plans these activities in order to support its policy and strategy and the effective operation of its processes

People 3e

Enablers | Results

Leadership → People / Policy and Strategy / Partnerships and Resources → Processes → People Results / Customer Results / Society Results → Key Performance Results

Innovation and Learning

The EFQM Excellence Model is a registered Trademark

3e People are rewarded, recognised and cared for

This may include:

How is reward and recognition used to encourage involvement in improvement and empower employees?

How is the work environment made conducive to encouraging employees to give of their best?

How are terms and conditions designed not only to recruit employees but also to focus on contributing to organisational improvement? Eg. childcare facilities

How are employees encouraged to take responsibility for managing and improving their work environment? e.g health and safety issues

How are reward systems and changes to work patterns achieved in line with organisational strategy and values?

How are employees encouraged to consider issues relating to the environment and society's needs in general?

Step 1. Assess importance of criterion

	These are not key issues	These issues are moderately important	These issues are important	These issues are critical
Importance Rating	(0)	(1)	(2)	(3)

Note: Tick a box to indicate your view of the importance of this criterion (note, the description of the criterion is the words after 3e)

Steps 2-5. Activity/Behaviour list

2. Activity /Behaviour	3. Duration of use	4. Deployment	5. How reviewed?

Step 2. List specific existing activities, policies, processes, behaviours and practices that impact on this criterion

Step 3. For each activity listed in step 2, list how long you have been using each policy, process or practice (years/months)

Step 4. List to what extent you want to deploy each policy, process and practice and how far they have been deployed to date

(eg by site, organisational level, department, activity, product etc)

Step 5. List how and how often you review the effectiveness of each activity and the overall process

Note: Annotate your comments onto the activity/behaviour list above

---

Step 6. List improvements resulting from reviews

Step 7. Review your comments on steps 1 to 6 as a whole, and form and record an opinion on the success of the **approaches** used, their **deployment** and the **review** of them. List this as a set of composite perceived strengths and areas for improvement. The scoring cards should be used to help your thoughts. The scoring card indicates which aspects of approach, deployment and review should influence your score.

Perceived strengths (+)	Perceived areas for improvement (–)

Note: List also areas for improvement relevant activities that you feel should be initiated and are not at present undertaken

Approach	%
Deployment	%
Assess & Review	%
Overall	%

You have now completed Criterion 3 - Note any actions required

4: Partnerships & Resources

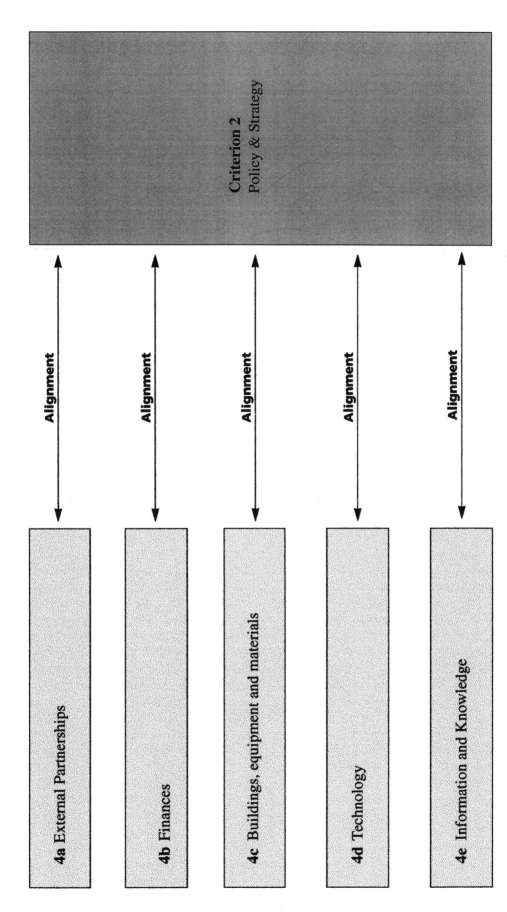

How the organisation plans and manages its external partnerships and internal resources in order to support its
policy and strategy and the effective operation of its processes

4a External partnerships are managed

This may include:

How does the organisation seek out and develop key partnerships to support its overall strategy?

How are the partnerships structured for maximum mutual benefit?

How are the partnerships focused on creating value for the joint customers?

How are the combined resources of the partnerships enhancing the potential for innovation and creativity through sharing knowledge?

Does the organisation take the lead in developing its key suppliers (and others in the supply chain) through partnership relationships?

Enablers — Results

Leadership | People | Partnerships and Resources | Processes | People Results | Customer Results | Society Results | Key Performance Results

Policy and Strategy

Innovation and Learning

The EFQM Excellence Model is a registered Trademark

Step 1. Assess importance of criterion

These are not key issues	These issues are moderately important	These issues are important	These issues are critical
(0)	(1)	(2)	(3)

Importance Rating

Note: Tick a box to indicate your view of the importance of this criterion (note, the description of the criterion is the words after 4a)

Steps 2-5. Activity/Behaviour list

2. Activity /Behaviour	3. Duration of use	4. Deployment	5. How reviewed?

Step 2. List specific existing activities, policies, processes, behaviours and practices that impact on this criterion

Step 3. For each activity listed in step 2, list how long you have been using each policy, process or practice (years/months)

Step 4. List to what extent you want to deploy each policy, process and practice and how far they have been deployed to date

    (eg by site, organisational level, department, activity, product etc)

Step 5. List how and how often you review the effectiveness of each activity and the overall process

Note: Annotate your comments onto the activity/behaviour list above

Step 6. List improvements resulting from reviews

Step 7. Review your comments on steps 1 to 6 as a whole, and form and record an opinion on the success of the **approaches** used, their **deployment** and the **review** of them. List this as a set of composite perceived strengths and areas for improvement. The scoring cards should be used to help your thoughts. The scoring card indicates which aspects of approach, deployment and review should influence your score.

Perceived strengths (+)	Perceived areas for improvement (-)

Approach	%
Deployment	%
Assess & Review	%
Overall	%

Note: List also areas for improvement relevant activities that you feel should be initiated and are not at present undertaken

125

How the organisation plans and manages its external partnerships and internal resources in order to support its policy and strategy and the effective operation of its processes

4b Finances are managed

This may include:

How does financial management support policy and strategy?

How are financial strategy and practices reviewed and improved?

How are financial mechanisms and parameters used to ensure an efficient and effective resourcing structure?

How are external controls on financial flexibility managed to allow maximum freedom within the organisation?

How are financial parameters such as cost, margins, value for money, assets, working capital, cash flow and profitability (if appropriate) managed for improvement?

How are investments evaluated?

How are financial management practices aligned to user needs?

How is financial risk managed?

Enablers / Results

Leadership — People, Policy and Strategy, Partnerships and Resources — Processes — People Results, Customer Results, Society Results — Key Performance Results

Innovation and Learning

The EFQM Excellence Model is a registered Trademark

Step 1. Assess importance of criterion

These are not key issues	These issues are moderately important	These issues are important	These issues are critical
(0)	(1)	(2)	(3)

Importance Rating

Note: Tick a box to indicate your view of the importance of this criterion (note, the description of the criterion is the words after 4b)

Steps 2-5. Activity/Behaviour list

2. Activity /Behaviour	3. Duration of use	4. Deployment	5. How reviewed?

Step 2. List specific existing activities, policies, processes, behaviours and practices that impact on this criterion

Step 3. For each activity listed in step 2, list how long you have been using each policy, process or practice (years/months)

Step 4. List to what extent you want to deploy each policy, process and practice and how far they have been deployed to date

(eg by site, organisational level, department, activity, product etc)

Step 5. List how and how often you review the effectiveness of each activity and the overall process

Note: Annotate your comments onto the activity/behaviour list above

Step 6. List improvements resulting from reviews

Step 7. Review your comments on steps 1 to 6 as a whole, and form and record an opinion on the success of the **approaches** used, their **deployment** and the **review** of them. List this as a set of composite perceived strengths and areas for improvement. The scoring cards should be used to help your thoughts. The scoring card indicates which aspects of approach, deployment and review should influence your score.

Perceived strengths (+)	Perceived areas for improvement (-)

Note: List also areas for improvement relevant activities that you feel should be initiated and are not at present undertaken

Approach	%
Deployment	%
Assess & Review	%
Overall	%

How the organisation plans and manages its external partnerships and internal resources in order to support its policy and strategy and the effective operation of its processes

Partnerships & Resources 4c

4c Buildings, equipment and materials are managed

This may include:

How are material inventories optimised?

How are assets optimised in support of policy and strategy?

How are the maintenance and utilisation of assets managed to improve total asset life cycle performance?

How is the impact of its assets on the community and employees (including health and safety) considered?

How is the security of assets managed?

How is waste reduced, recycled and minimised?

How are global non-renewable resources conserved?

How is any adverse global impact of the organisation's products and services considered and reduced?

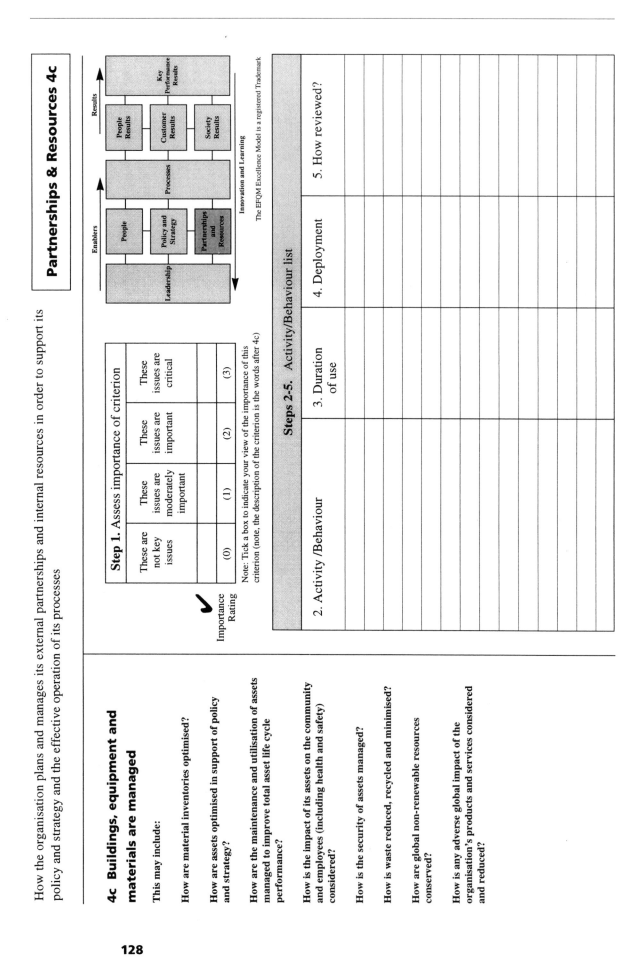

The EFQM Excellence Model is a registered Trademark

Step 1. Assess importance of criterion

	These are not key issues	These issues are moderately important	These issues are important	These issues are critical
Importance Rating	(0)	(1)	(2)	(3)

Note: Tick a box to indicate your view of the importance of this criterion (note, the description of the criterion is the words after 4c)

Steps 2-5. Activity/Behaviour list

2. Activity /Behaviour	3. Duration of use	4. Deployment	5. How reviewed?

Step 2. List specific existing activities, policies, processes, behaviours and practices that impact on this criterion

Step 3. For each activity listed in step 2, list how long you have been using each policy, process or practice (years/months)

Step 4. List to what extent you want to deploy each policy, process and practice and how far they have been deployed to date
(eg by site, organisational level, department, activity, product etc)

Step 5. List how and how often you review the effectiveness of each activity and the overall process

Note: Annotate your comments onto the activity/behaviour list above

Step 6. List improvements resulting from reviews

Step 7. Review your comments on steps 1 to 6 as a whole, and form and record an opinion on the success of the **approaches** used, their **deployment** and the **review** of them. List this as a set of composite perceived strengths and areas for improvement. The scoring cards should be used to help your thoughts. The scoring card indicates which aspects of approach, deployment and review should influence your score.

Perceived strengths (+)

Perceived areas for improvement (-)

Note: List also areas for improvement relevant activities that you feel should be initiated and are not at present undertaken

Approach	%
Deployment	%
Assess & Review	%
Overall	%

How the organisation plans and manages its external partnerships and internal resources in order to support its policy and strategy and the effective operation of its processes

Partnerships & Resources 4d

Enablers | Results

Innovation and Learning

The EFQM Excellence Model is a registered Trademark

4d Technology is managed

This may include:

How has existing technology been exploited?

How are the processes of technology management aligned to the organisation's strategies?

How are alternative and emerging technologies identified and evaluated in the light of policy and strategy and their possible impact on the organisation and society?

How are technologies developed as the basis of the organisation's operations and services?

How are the skills and capabilities of the people harmonised with developing technology?

How is technology harnessed in support of process, information systems and other systems improvement?

Step 1. Assess importance of criterion

	These are not key issues	These issues are moderately important	These issues are important	These issues are critical
Importance Rating	(0)	(1)	(2)	(3)

Note: Tick a box to indicate your view of the importance of this criterion (note, the description of the criterion is the words after 4d)

Steps 2-5. Activity/Behaviour list

2. Activity /Behaviour	3. Duration of use	4. Deployment	5. How reviewed?

Step 2. List specific existing activities, policies, processes, behaviours and practices that impact on this criterion

Step 3. For each activity listed in step 2, list how long you have been using each policy, process or practice (years/months)

Step 4. List to what extent you want to deploy each policy, process and practice and how far they have been deployed to date
(eg by site, organisational level, department, activity, product etc)

Step 5. List how and how often you review the effectiveness of each activity and the overall process

Note: Annotate your comments onto the activity/behaviour list above

Step 6. List improvements resulting from reviews

Step 7. Review your comments on steps 1 to 6 as a whole, and form and record an opinion on the success of the **approaches** used, their **deployment** and the **review** of them. List this as a set of composite perceived strengths and areas for improvement. The scoring cards should be used to help your thoughts. The scoring card indicates which aspects of approach, deployment and review should influence your score.

Perceived strengths (+)

Perceived areas for improvement (-)

Approach	%
Deployment	%
Assess & Review	%
Overall	%

Note: List also areas for improvement relevant activities that you feel should be initiated and are not at present undertaken

131

How the organisation plans and manages its external partnerships and internal resources in order to support its policy and strategy and the effective operation of its processes

4e Information and knowledge are managed

This may include:

How is knowledge as well as data and information focused on meeting the needs of the organisation and its customers?

How are information and knowledge used to stimulate innovation and creativity?

How are information systems managed to reflect user needs?

How is information made accessible to those who need it and how are these needs determined from customers, suppliers, people,etc

How are information strategies and the underlying processes of information management aligned to policy and strategy?

How is information validity, availability, integrity and security/confidentiality assured and improved?

How are operational and service improvements achieved through the use of information resources?

Enablers — Results

Leadership | People | Policy and Strategy | Partnerships and Resources | Processes | People Results | Customer Results | Society Results | Key Performance Results

Innovation and Learning

The EFQM Excellence Model is a registered Trademark

Step 1. Assess importance of criterion

	These are not key issues	These issues are moderately important	These issues are important	These issues are critical
	(0)	(1)	(2)	(3)
Importance Rating				

Note: Tick a box to indicate your view of the importance of this criterion (note, the description of the criterion is the words after 4e)

Steps 2-5. Activity/Behaviour list

2. Activity /Behaviour	3. Duration of use	4. Deployment	5. How reviewed?

Step 2. List specific existing activities, policies, processes, behaviours and practices that impact on this criterion

Step 3. For each activity listed in step 2, list how long you have been using each policy, process or practice (years/months)

Step 4. List to what extent you want to deploy each policy, process and practice and how far they have been deployed to date

(eg by site, organisational level, department, activity, product etc)

Step 5. List how and how often you review the effectiveness of each activity and the overall process

Note: Annotate your comments onto the activity/behaviour list above

Step 6. List improvements resulting from reviews

Step 7. Review your comments on steps 1 to 6 as a whole, and form and record an opinion on the success of the **approaches** used, their **deployment** and the **review** of them. List this as a set of composite perceived strengths and areas for improvement. The scoring cards should be used to help your thoughts. The scoring card indicates which aspects of approach, deployment and review should influence your score.

Perceived strengths (+)	Perceived areas for improvement (–)

Note: List also areas for improvement relevant activities that you feel should be initiated and are not at present undertaken

Approach	%
Deployment	%
Assess & Review	%
Overall	%

133

You have now completed Criterion 4 - Note any actions required

5: Processes

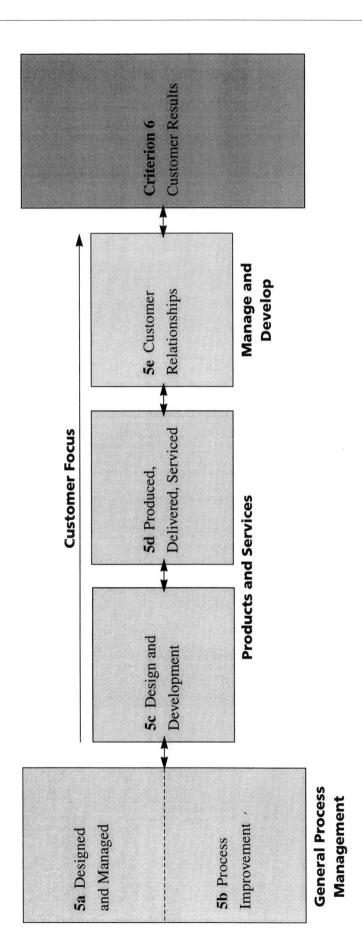

General Process Management

5a Designed and Managed

5b Process Improvement

Products and Services

5c Design and Development

5d Produced, Delivered, Serviced

Manage and Develop

5e Customer Relationships

Customer Focus

Criterion 6
Customer Results

How the organisation designs, manages and improves its processes in order to support its policy and strategy and fully satisfy, and generate increasing value for, its customers and other stakeholders

Enablers

Results

Leadership → People, Policy and Strategy, Partnerships and Resources → Processes → People Results, Customer Results, Society Results → Key Performance Results

Innovation and Learning

The EFQM Excellence Model is a registered Trademark

5a Processes are systematically designed and managed

This may include:

Does the organisation have a system to ensure that all the processes are managed and controlled against appropriate standards?

Are there measures in place for all processes?

Is the capability of processes measured as well as their output?

How are interface issues addressed across functional boundaries and externally?

How are system standards considered and applied to process management e.g. for quality, environment, health and safety?

How is the process management structure designed to deliver the organisation's overall strategy?

Step 1. Assess importance of criterion

	These are not key issues	These issues are moderately important	These issues are important	These issues are critical
Importance Rating	(0)	(1)	(2)	(3)

Note: Tick a box to indicate your view of the importance of this criterion (note, the description of the criterion is the words after 5a)

Steps 2-5. Activity/Behaviour list

2. Activity /Behaviour	3. Duration of use	4. Deployment	5. How reviewed?

Step 2. List specific existing activities, policies, processes, behaviours and practices that impact on this criterion

Step 3. For each activity listed in step 2, list how long you have been using each policy, process or practice (years/months)

Step 4. List to what extent you want to deploy each policy, process and practice and how far they have been deployed to date

(eg by site, organisational level, department, activity, product etc)

Step 5. List how and how often you review the effectiveness of each activity and the overall process

Note: Annotate your comments onto the activity/behaviour list above

Step 6. List improvements resulting from reviews

Step 7. Review your comments on steps 1 to 6 as a whole, and form and record an opinion on the success of the **approaches** used, their **deployment** and the **review** of them. List this as a set of composite perceived strengths and areas for improvement. The scoring cards should be used to help your thoughts. The scoring card indicates which aspects of approach, deployment and review should influence your score.

Perceived strengths (+)	Perceived areas for improvement (-)

Note: List also areas for improvement relevant activities that you feel should be initiated and are not at present undertaken

Approach	%
Deployment	%
Assess & Review	%
Overall	%

137

How the organisation designs, manages and improves its processes in order to support its policy and strategy and fully satisfy, and generate increasing value for, its customers and other stakeholders

Enablers | Results

Leadership → People, Policy and Strategy, Partnerships and Resources → Processes → People Results, Customer Results, Society Results → Key Performance Results

Innovation and Learning

The EFQM Excellence Model is a registered Trademark

Step 1. Assess importance of criterion

	These are not key issues	These issues are moderately important	These issues are important	These issues are critical
Importance Rating	(0)	(1)	(2)	(3)

Note: Tick a box to indicate your view of the importance of this criterion (note, the description of the criterion is the words after 5b)

Steps 2-5. Activity/Behaviour list

2. Activity /Behaviour	3. Duration of use	4. Deployment	5. How reviewed?

5b Processes are improved, as needed, using innovation in order to fully satisfy and generate increasing value for customers and other stakeholders

This may include:

How are decisions taken to set priorities for both continuous improvement and step change? How is the balance of these activities reviewed?

Are current performance measurements and improvement targets related to past achievement to ensure they are realistic?

How is data from best-in-class organisations, and other benchmarking sources, used to set stretch targets? How are these aligned to business goals?

How are new principles of design, technologies, and operating philosophies proactively identified, appraised and introduced for process improvement?

How is innovation and creativity in process improvement stimulated?

Are process/project improvements piloted and proved before implementation?

How is implementation of change controlled?

How does the organisation communicate the details of process change to all appropriate stakeholders?

How does the organisation identify any training needed to implement the changes?

Does the organisation carry out post-implementation assessment of whether changes achieved predicted benefits?

Step 2. List specific existing activities, policies, processes, behaviours and practices that impact on this criterion

Step 3. For each activity listed in step 2, list how long you have been using each policy, process or practice (years/months)

Step 4. List to what extent you want to deploy each policy, process and practice and how far they have been deployed to date
(eg by site, organisational level, department, activity, product etc)

Step 5. List how and how often you review the effectiveness of each activity and the overall process

Note: Annotate your comments onto the activity/behaviour list above

Step 6. List improvements resulting from reviews

Step 7. Review your comments on steps 1 to 6 as a whole, and form and record an opinion on the success of the **approaches** used, their **deployment** and the **review** of them. List this as a set of composite perceived strengths and areas for improvement. The scoring cards should be used to help your thoughts. The scoring card indicates which aspects of approach, deployment and review should influence your score.

Perceived strengths (+)	Perceived areas for improvement (-)

Note: List also areas for improvement relevant activities that you feel should be initiated and are not at present undertaken

Approach	%
Deployment	%
Assess & Review	%
Overall	%

How the organisation designs, manages and improves its processes in order to support its policy and strategy and fully satisfy, and generate increasing value for, its customers and other stakeholders

The EFQM Excellence Model is a registered Trademark

5c Products and services are designed and developed based on customer needs and expectations

This may include:

How are the market and specific customer needs for products and services identified?

How are the future needs anticipated for either new products and services or improvements to existing ones?

How are design and development activities focused on customer needs and expectations?

How does the organisation aim for a competitive edge by using innovation and creativity in its development process?

How does the organisation work in partnership to develop new products and services?

Step 1. Assess importance of criterion

	These are not key issues	These issues are moderately important	These issues are important	These issues are critical
Importance Rating	(0)	(1)	(2)	(3)

Note: Tick a box to indicate your view of the importance of this criterion (note, the description of the criterion is the words after 5c)

Steps 2-5. Activity/Behaviour list

2. Activity /Behaviour	3. Duration of use	4. Deployment	5. How reviewed?

Step 2. List specific existing activities, policies, processes, behaviours and practices that impact on this criterion

Step 3. For each activity listed in step 2, list how long you have been using each policy, process or practice (years/months)

Step 4. List to what extent you want to deploy each policy, process and practice and how far they have been deployed to date
(eg by site, organisational level, department, activity, product etc)

Step 5. List how and how often you review the effectiveness of each activity and the overall process

Note: Annotate your comments onto the activity/behaviour list above

Step 6. List improvements resulting from reviews

Step 7. Review your comments on steps 1 to 6 as a whole, and form and record an opinion on the success of the **approaches** used, their **deployment** and the **review** of them. List this as a set of composite perceived strengths and areas for improvement. The scoring cards should be used to help your thoughts. The scoring card indicates which aspects of approach, deployment and review should influence your score.

Perceived strengths (+)	Perceived areas for improvement (−)

Note: List also areas for improvement relevant activities that you feel should be initiated and are not at present undertaken

Approach	%
Deployment	%
Assess & Review	%
Overall	%

How the organisation designs, manages and improves its processes in order to support its policy and strategy and fully satisfy, and generate increasing value for, its customers and other stakeholders

---

Processes 5d

The EFQM Excellence Model is a registered Trademark

5d Products and Services are produced, delivered and serviced

This may include:

What is the approach to producing products and services to meet the defined design requirements?

How does the organisation decide whether to outsource products and services to meet defined requirements?

How are existing and new customers and the market generally made aware of the organisation's products and services?

How are customers provided with the products and services to meet their needs?

How is the after sales process managed?

Step 1. Assess importance of criterion

	These are not key issues	These issues are moderately important	These issues are important	These issues are critical
Importance Rating	(0)	(1)	(2)	(3)

Note: Tick a box to indicate your view of the importance of this criterion (note, the description of the criterion is the words after 5d)

Steps 2-5. Activity/Behaviour list

2. Activity /Behaviour	3. Duration of use	4. Deployment	5. How reviewed?

Step 2. List specific existing activities, policies, processes, behaviours and practices that impact on this criterion

Step 3. For each activity listed in step 2, list how long you have been using each policy, process or practice (years/months)

Step 4. List to what extent you want to deploy each policy, process and practice and how far they have been deployed to date

(eg by site, organisational level, department, activity, product etc)

Step 5. List how and how often you review the effectiveness of each activity and the overall process

Note: Annotate your comments onto the activity/behaviour list above

Step 6. List improvements resulting from reviews

Step 7. Review your comments on steps 1 to 6 as a whole, and form and record an opinion on the success of the **approaches** used, their **deployment** and the **review** of them. List this as a set of composite perceived strengths and areas for improvement. The scoring cards should be used to help your thoughts. The scoring card indicates which aspects of approach, deployment and review should influence your score.

Perceived strengths (+)	Perceived areas for improvement (-)

Note: List also areas for improvement relevant activities that you feel should be initiated and are not at present undertaken

Approach	%
Deployment	%
Assess & Review	%
Overall	%

How the organisation designs, manages and improves its processes in order to support its policy and strategy and fully satisfy, and generate increasing value for, its customers and other stakeholders

The EFQM Excellence Model is a registered Trademark

5e Customer relationships are managed and enhanced

This may include:

How are customer contact needs established and met?

How does the organisation take and respond to routine customer feedback, both positive and negative?

How does the organisation take the lead in establishing and meeting the needs for its relationships with its customers?

How are the various points in the customer contact process monitored and then responded to in order to improve the ongoing relationship?

How does the organisation plan and structure its approach to gathering specific customer feedback relevant to the issues that influence their satisfaction with the relationship?

How is customer feedback used to manage and improve the relationship?

Step 1. Assess importance of criterion

	These are not key issues	These issues are moderately important	These issues are important	These issues are critical
Importance Rating	(0)	(1)	(2)	(3)

Note: Tick a box to indicate your view of the importance of this criterion (note, the description of the criterion is the words after 5e)

Steps 2-5. Activity/Behaviour list

2. Activity /Behaviour	3. Duration of use	4. Deployment	5. How reviewed?

Step 2. List specific existing activities, policies, processes, behaviours and practices that impact on this criterion

Step 3. For each activity listed in step 2, list how long you have been using each policy, process or practice (years/months)

Step 4. List to what extent you want to deploy each policy, process and practice and how far they have been deployed to date

(eg by site, organisational level, department, activity, product etc)

Step 5. List how and how often you review the effectiveness of each activity and the overall process

Note: Annotate your comments onto the activity/behaviour list above

Step 6. List improvements resulting from reviews

Step 7. Review your comments on steps 1 to 6 as a whole, and form and record an opinion on the success of the **approaches** used, their **deployment** and the **review** of them. List this as a set of composite perceived strengths and areas for improvement. The scoring cards should be used to help your thoughts. The scoring card indicates which aspects of approach, deployment and review should influence your score.

Perceived strengths (+)	Perceived areas for improvement (-)

Note: List also areas for improvement relevant activities that you feel should be initiated and are not at present undertaken

Approach	%
Deployment	%
Assess & Review	%
Overall	%

You have now completed Criterion 5 - Note any actions required

6: Customer Results

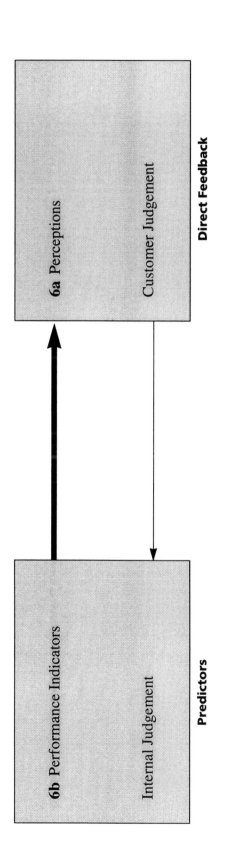

6a Perceptions

Customer Judgement

Direct Feedback

6b Performance Indicators

Internal Judgement

Predictors

Measuring:

Overall Image
Products & Services
Sales & After Sales
Loyalty

What the organisation is achieving in relation to its external customers

The EFQM Excellence Model is a registered Trademark

6a Perception measures
(from surveys,focus groups,vendor ratings and complaints)

Depending on the purpose of the organisation, customer perception measures may include those relating to:

Organisation image
- accessibility and communication
- flexibility and responsiveness
- being pro-active

Products and services
- quality and delivery
- value for money
- reliability
- design and innovation
- environmentally friendly

Ongoing support
- customer focus of employees
- advice and technical support
- customer literature and technical documentation
- handling complaints, warranty and guarantees
- product training
- response time

Loyalty
- intention to come back
- willingness to purchase other products and services
- willingness to refer other customers to the organisation

Step 1. Assess importance of criterion

	These are not key issues	These issues are moderately important	These issues are important	These issues are critical
Importance Rating	(0)	(1)	(2)	(3)

Note: Tick a box to indicate your view of the importance of this criterion (note, the description of the criterion is the words after 6a)

Steps 2-6. Data/Measure List

2. Data/Measures Used	3. Trend (+/0/-)	4. Duration of Trend (yrs)	5. Comparison with targets (+/0/-)	6. Comparison with competitors and/or best in class (+/0/-)

Step 2 List the data/measures that you use

Step 3. Note which data recorded in step 2 are showing positive or negative trends

Step 4. Note the duration of the trends

Step 5. Note which data are meeting or exceeding the targets you set

Step 6. Assess the relationship of your results with competitors and/or best in class organisations and list your key successes

Note: Annotate your comments onto the list from step 2

Step 7. List any results that you perceive to be relevant to customers that are not covered by data

Step 8. Form and record an opinion on the scope, trends, levels and comparisons of your performance. List this as perceived strengths and areas for improvement. The scoring cards may help in the process, and indicate which aspects of **Results** and **Scope** should influence your thinking

Perceived strengths (+)	Perceived areas for improvement (-)

Note: List any relevant measures or comparisons that you feel should be initiated, and are not at present undertaken, as areas for improvement

Results	%
Scope	%
Overall	%

149

What the organisation is achieving in relation to its external customers

Customer Results 6b

6b Performance Indicators (internal predictor measures)

Depending on the purpose of the organisation, performance indicators for customers may include those relating to:

Organisation image
- number of customer accolades and awards
- press coverage and other media

Products and services
- competitiveness
- defect, error and rejection rates
- levels of complaints, guarantees and warranty claims
- delays
- product life cycle
- design innovation and time to market

Ongoing support
- demand for training
- handling of complaints
- response rates

Repeat business
- duration of relationship and customer retention
- frequency/value of orders
- lifetime value
- new and/or lost business
- number/value of referrals

Enablers — Results

Leadership — People, Policy and Strategy, Partnerships and Resources — Processes — People Results, Customer Results, Society Results — Key Performance Results

Innovation and Learning

The EFQM Excellence Model is a registered Trademark

Step 1. Assess importance of criterion			
	These are not key issues	These issues are moderately important	These issues are important	These issues are critical
Importance Rating	(0)	(1)	(2)	(3)

Note: Tick a box to indicate your view of the importance of this criterion (note, the description of the criterion is the words after 6b)

Steps 2-6. Data/Measure List

2. Data/Measures Used	3. Trend (+/0/-)	4. Duration of Trend (yrs)	5. Comparison with targets (+/0/-)	6. Comparison with competitors and/or best in class (+/0/-)

Step 2 List the data/measures that you use

Step 3. Note which data recorded in step 2 are showing positive or negative trends

Step 4. Note the duration of the trends

Step 5. Note which data are meeting or exceeding the targets you set

Step 6. Assess the relationship of your results with competitors and/or best in class organisations and list your key successes

Note: Annotate your comments onto the list from step 2

Step 7. List any results that you perceive to be relevant to customers that are not covered by data

Step 8. Form and record an opinion on the scope, trends, levels and comparisons of your performance. List this as perceived strengths and areas for improvement. The scoring cards may help in the process, and indicate which aspects of **Results** and **Scope** should influence your thinking

Perceived strengths (+)	Perceived areas for improvement (-)

Results	%
Scope	%
Overall	%

Note: List any relevant measures or comparisons that you feel should be initiated, and are not at present undertaken, as areas for improvement

You have now completed Criterion 6 - Note any actions required

7: People Results

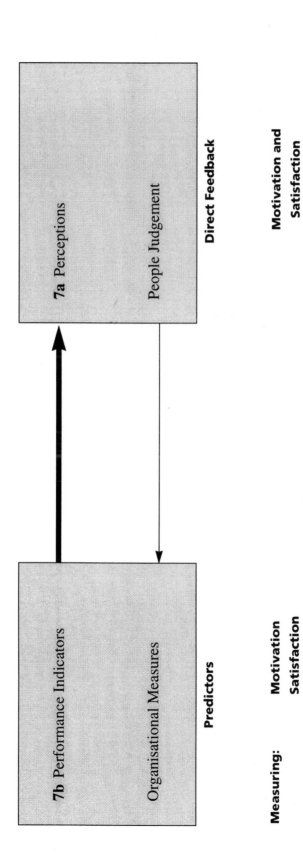

7a Perceptions

People Judgement

Direct Feedback

Motivation and

Satisfaction

7b Performance Indicators

Organisational Measures

Predictors

Measuring: **Motivation**
Satisfaction
Achievements
Services Provided

What the organisation is achieving in relation to its people

7a Perception Measures
(from surveys, focus groups, interviews and appraisals)

People perception measures may include:

Motivating factors
- career development and opportunities to achieve
- communication
- involvement and empowerment
- equal opportunities
- leadership issues
- recognition
- target setting and appraisal
- values, mission, vision, policy and strategy
- learning, training and development

Satisfaction measures
- organisation's administration
- employment conditions, pay and benefits
- job security and the management of change
- health and safety and working environment
- peer relationships
- impact of environmental policy
- the organisation's role in the community

The EFQM Excellence Model is a registered Trademark

Step 1. Assess importance of criterion			
	These are not key issues	These issues are moderately important	These issues are important	These issues are critical
Importance Rating	(0)	(1)	(2)	(3)

Note: Tick a box to indicate your view of the importance of this criterion (note, the description of the criterion is the words after 7a)

Steps 2-6. Data/Measure List

2. Data/Measures Used	3. Trend (+/0/-)	4. Duration of Trend (yrs)	5. Comparison with targets (+/0/-)	6. Comparison with competitors and/or best in class (+/0/-)

Step 2 List the data/measures that you use

Step 3. Note which data recorded in step 2 are showing positive or negative trends

Step 4. Note the duration of the trends

Step 5. Note which data are meeting or exceeding the targets you set

Step 6. Assess the relationship of your results with competitors and/or best in class organisations and list your key successes

Note: Annotate your comments onto the list from step 2

Step 7. List any results that you perceive to be relevant to your employees that are not covered by data

Step 8. Form and record an opinion on the scope, trends, levels and comparisons of your performance. List this as perceived strengths and areas for improvement. The scoring cards may help in the process, and indicate which aspects of **Results** and **Scope** should influence your thinking

Perceived areas for improvement (-)

Perceived strengths (+)

Note: List any relevant measures or comparisons that you feel should be initiated, and are not at present undertaken, as areas for improvement

Results	%
Scope	%
Overall	%

What the organisation is achieving in relation to its people

7b Performance Indicators (internal predictor measures)

Depending on the purpose of the organisation, performance indicators for people may include those relating to:

Employee achievements
- competency requirements versus those available
- productivity
- success of training and development to meet objectives

Evidence of participation
- involvement in improvement teams and suggestion schemes
- trends of training and development
- measurable benefits of team work
- recognition of individuals and teams
- response rates to people surveys.

Satisfaction indicators
- accident, absenteeism and sickness levels
- grievances and strikes
- staff turnover and recruitment trends
- use of benefits and organisation provided facilities (e.g. recreational, creche)

Organisation provided services
- accuracy of personnel administration
- communication effectiveness
- enquiries response time
- training evaluation

Step 1. Assess importance of criterion

	These are not key issues	These issues are moderately important	These issues are important	These issues are critical
	(0)	(1)	(2)	(3)
Importance Rating				

Note: Tick a box to indicate your view of the importance of this criterion (note, the description of the criterion is the words after 7b)

Steps 2-6. Data/Measure List

2. Data/Measures Used	3. Trend (+/0/-)	4. Duration of Trend (yrs)	5. Comparison with targets (+/0/-)	6. Comparison with competitors and/or best in class (+/0/-)

Enablers — Results

Leadership | People | Policy and Strategy | Partnerships and Resources | Processes | People Results | Customer Results | Society Results | Key Performance Results

Innovation and Learning

The EFQM Excellence Model is a registered Trademark

Step 2 List the data/measures that you use

Step 3. Note which data recorded in step 2 are showing positive or negative trends

Step 4. Note the duration of the trends

Step 5. Note which data are meeting or exceeding the targets you set

Step 6. Assess the relationship of your results with competitors and/or best in class organisations and list your key successes

Note: Annotate your comments onto the list from step 2

Step 7. List any results that you perceive to be relevant to customers that are not covered by data

Step 8. Form and record an opinion on the scope, trends, levels and comparisons of your performance. List this as perceived strengths and areas for improvement. The scoring cards may help in the process, and indicate which aspects of **Results** and **Scope** should influence your thinking

Perceived strengths (+)	Perceived areas for improvement (-)

Note: List any relevant measures or comparisons that you feel should be initiated, and are not at present undertaken, as areas for improvement

Results	%
Scope	%
Overall	%

You have now completed Criterion 7 - Note any actions required

8: Society Results

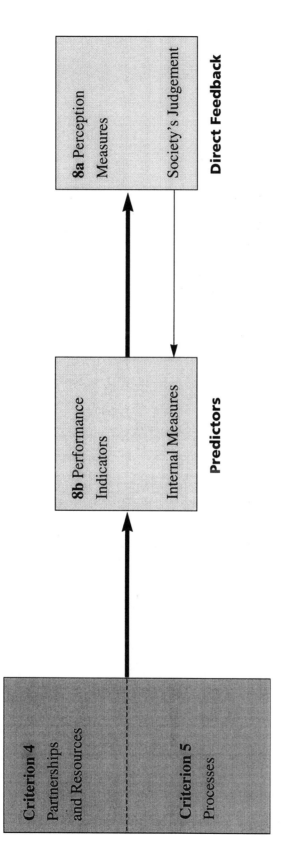

- **Responsible Citizen**
- **Community Involvement**
- **Prevent Nuisance**
- **Preserve Resources**

8a Perception Measures

Society's Judgement

Direct Feedback

8b Performance Indicators

Internal Measures

Predictors

Criterion 4
Partnerships and Resources

Criterion 5
Processes

What the organisation is achieving in relation to local, national and international society as appropriate

Enablers | Results

Leadership · People · Policy and Strategy · Partnerships and Resources · Processes

People Results · Customer Results · Society Results · Key Performance Results

Innovation and Learning

The EFQM Excellence Model is a registered Trademark

8a Perception Measures (from surveys, reports, public representatives and meetings, and authorities)

Depending on the purpose of the organisation, society perception measures may include those relating to:

Corporate citizenship
- disclosures of information relevant to the community
- equal opportunities practices
- impact on local and national economies
- relationships with relevant authorities
- ethical behaviour

Supporting the local community
- education and training
- medical and welfare provision
- sport and leisure
- voluntary work and philanthropy

Impact of its operations and/or products throughout the lifecycle
- health risks and accidents
- noise and odour
- safety hazards
- pollution and toxic emission
- used product disposal

The preservation and sustainability of resources
- choice of transport
- ecological impact
- reduction and elimination of waste and packaging
- substitution of raw materials or other inputs
- usage of utilities e.g. gases, water, electricity, new and recycled materials

Step 1. Assess importance of criterion

	These are not key issues	These issues are moderately important	These issues are important	These issues are critical
Importance Rating	(0)	(1)	(2)	(3)

Note: Tick a box to indicate your view of the importance of this criterion (note, the description of the criterion is the words after 8a)

Steps 2-6. Data/Measure List

2. Data/Measures Used	3. Trend (+/0/-)	4. Duration of Trend (yrs)	5. Comparison with targets (+/0/-)	6. Comparison with competitors and/or best in class (+/0/-)

Step 2 List the data/measures that you use

Step 3. Note which data recorded in step 2 are showing positive or negative trends

Step 4. Note the duration of the trends

Step 5. Note which data are meeting or exceeding the targets you set

Step 6. Assess the relationship of your results with competitors and/or best in class organisations and list your key successes

Note: Annotate your comments onto the list from step 2

Step 7. List any results that you perceive to be relevant to society that are not covered by data

Step 8. Form and record an opinion on the scope, trends, levels and comparisons of your performance. List this as perceived strengths and areas for improvement. The scoring cards may help in the process, and indicate which aspects of **Results** and **Scope** should influence your thinking

Perceived strengths (+)	Perceived areas for improvement (-)

Note: List any relevant measures or comparisons that you feel should be initiated, and are not at present undertaken, as areas for improvement

Results	%
Scope	%
Overall	%

What the organisation is achieving in relation to local, national and international society as appropriate

8b Performance Indicators (internal predictor measures)

Depending on the purpose of the organisation, performance indicators for society may include those listed under 8a and in addition:

- handling of changes in employment levels
- use of formal management systems particularly in relation to environmental management and audit
- dealings of the organisation with authorities in relation to new services, planning etc
- press coverage
- accolades and awards received

Internal measures of - trends of active involvement in community support such as charity support, participation in community events, involvement in education and training, volunteering, environmental and ecological improvement activity, medical welfare activities and sports and leisure activities

Internal measures of trends in activities to reduce and prevent nuisance and harm to neighbours as a result of operations, business related transportation and products, eg noise and pollution reduction activities, vehicle access, hazards and health risk management

Internal measures of trends and activities to assist the preservation of global resources such as energy, material resources, conservation, use of recycled material, reduction of waste, recycling, environmental and ecological impact issues

Step 1. Assess importance of criterion

	These are not key issues	These issues are moderately important	These issues are important	These issues are critical
Importance Rating	(0)	(1)	(2)	(3)

Note: Tick a box to indicate your view of the importance of this criterion (note, the description of the criterion is the words after 8b)

Steps 2-6. Data/Measure List

2. Data/Measures Used	3. Trend (+/0/-)	4. Duration of Trend (yrs)	5. Comparison with targets (+/0/-)	6. Comparison with competitors and/or best in class (+/0/-)

Enablers

Leadership · People · Policy and Strategy · Partnerships and Resources · Processes

Results

People Results · Customer Results · Society Results · Key Performance Results

Innovation and Learning

The EFQM Excellence Model is a registered Trademark

Step 2 List the data/measures that you use

Step 3. Note which data recorded in step 2 are showing positive or negative trends

Step 4. Note the duration of the trends

Step 5. Note which data are meeting or exceeding the targets you set

Step 6. Assess the relationship of your results with competitors and/or best in class organisations and list your key successes

Note: Annotate your comments onto the list from step 2

Step 7. List any results that you perceive to be relevant to society that are not covered by data

Step 8. Form and record an opinion on the scope, trends, levels and comparisons of your performance. List this as perceived strengths and areas for improvement. The scoring cards may help in the process, and indicate which aspects of **Results** and **Scope** should influence your thinking

Perceived strengths (+)	Perceived areas for improvement (-)

Note: List any relevant measures or comparisons that you feel should be initiated, and are not at present undertaken, as areas for improvement

Results	%
Scope	%
Overall	%

You have now completed Criterion 8 - Note any actions required

9: Key Performance Results

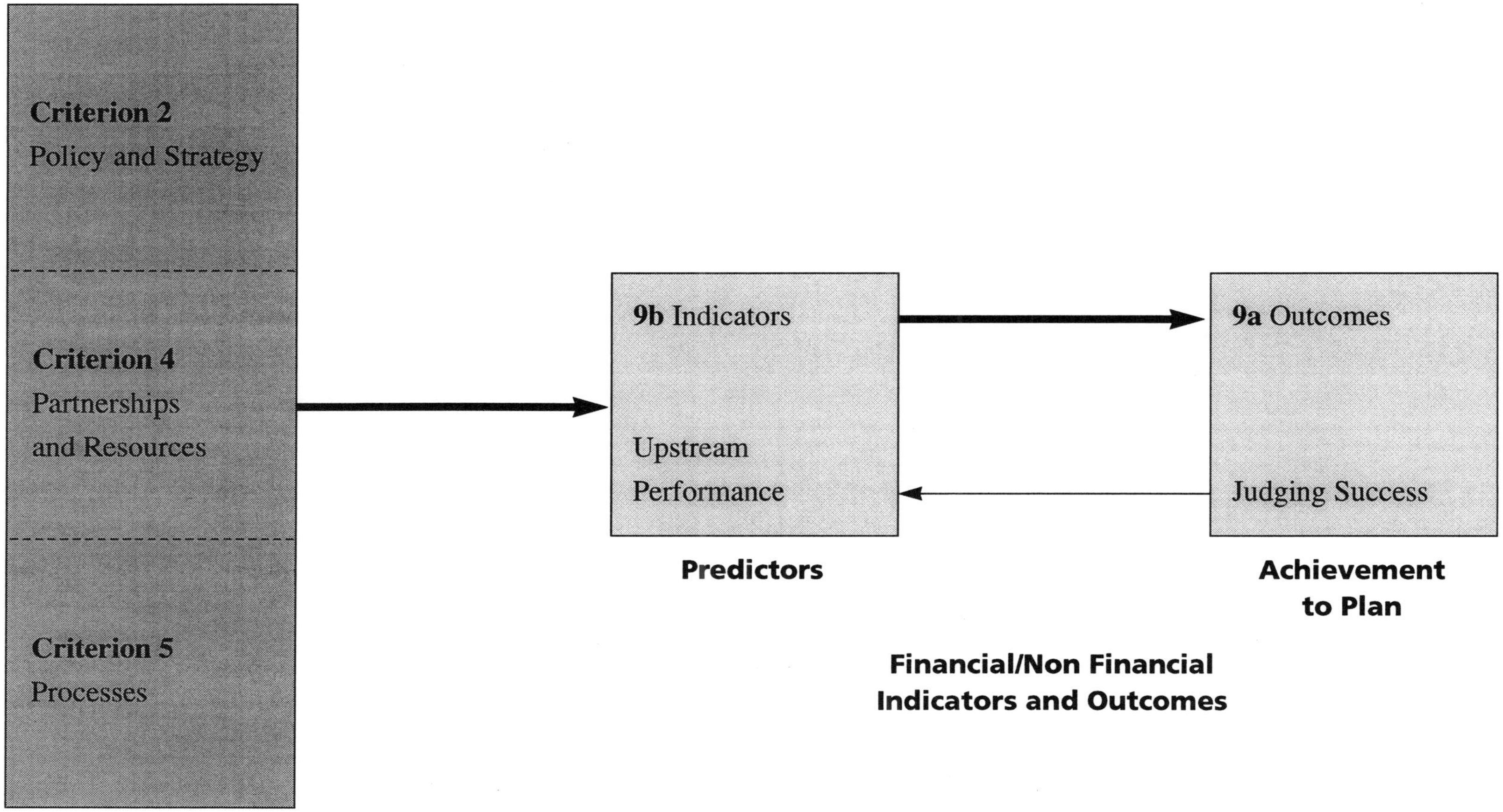

What the organisation is achieving in relation to its planned performance

The EFQM Excellence Model is a registered Trademark

9a Key performance outcomes

These measures are key results planned by the organisation and which, depending on the purpose and objectives of the organisation, may include those relating to:

Financial outcomes
- share price and dividends
- gross and net profit
- sales
- meeting of budgets

Non-financial outcomes
- market share
- time to market
- volumes
- success rates

Step 1. Assess importance of criterion

	These are not key issues	These issues are moderately important	These issues are important	These issues are critical
Importance Rating	(0)	(1)	(2)	(3)

Note: Tick a box to indicate your view of the importance of this criterion (note, the description of the criterion is the words after 9a)

Steps 2-6. Data/Measure List

2. Data/Measures Used	3. Trend (+/0/-)	4. Duration of Trend (yrs)	5. Comparison with targets (+/0/-)	6. Comparison with competitors and/or best in class (+/0/-)

Step 2 List the data/measures that you use

Step 3. Note which data recorded in step 2 are showing positive or negative trends

Step 4. Note the duration of the trends

Step 5. Note which data are meeting or exceeding the targets you set

Step 6. Assess the relationship of your results with competitors and/or best in class organisations and list your key successes

Note: Annotate your comments onto the list from step 2

Step 7. List any results that you perceive to be relevant to your stakeholders that are not covered by data

Step 8. Form and record an opinion on the scope, trends, levels and comparisons of your performance. List this as perceived strengths and areas for improvement. The scoring cards may help in the process, and indicate which aspects of **Results** and **Scope** should influence your thinking

Perceived strengths (+)	Perceived areas for improvement (-)

Note: List any relevant measures or comparisons that you feel should be initiated, and are not at present undertaken, as areas for improvement

Results	%
Scope	%
Overall	%

9b Key performance indicators

These measures are the operational ones used in order to monitor, understand, predict and improve the organisation's likely key performance outcomes. Depending on the purpose and objectives of the organisation and its processes, they may include those reating to:

Internal process measures

- performance and productivity, assessments, innovations and improvements, cycle times, defect rate, maturity and deployment, time to market

External resources including partnerships

- supplier price and performance, number and value add of partnerships, number and value add of innovative products and services, solutions generated by partners, number and value add of joint improvements with partners, recognition of partners' contribution

Financial

- cash flow items, balance sheet items, depreciation and maintenance costs, return on net assets and equity, credit ratings

Buildings, equipment and materials

- defect rates and shortages, inventory turnover, utility consumption, utilisation, service disruption

Technology

- innovation rate, value of intellectual property, patents and royalties

Information and knowledge

- integrity and accuracy, accessibility, relevance and timeliness, sharing and using knowledge and value of intellectual capital

---

The EFQM Excellence Model is a registered Trademark

Step 1. Assess importance of criterion

	These are not key issues	These issues are moderately important	These issues are important	These issues are critical
Importance Rating	(0)	(1)	(2)	(3)

Note: Tick a box to indicate your view of the importance of this criterion (note, the description of the criterion is the words after 9b)

Steps 2-6. Data/Measure List

2. Data/Measures Used	3. Trend (+/0/-)	4. Duration of Trend (yrs)	5. Comparison with targets (+/0/-)	6. Comparison with competitors and/or best in class (+/0/-)

Step 2 List the data/measures that you use

Step 3. Note which data recorded in step 2 are showing positive or negative trends

Step 4. Note the duration of the trends

Step 5. Note which data are meeting or exceeding the targets you set

Step 6. Assess the relationship of your results with competitors and/or best in class organisations and list your key successes

Note: Annotate your comments onto the list from step 2

Step 7. List any results that you perceive to be relevant to your stakeholders that are not covered by data

Step 8. Form and record an opinion on the scope, trends, levels and comparisons of your performance. List this as perceived strengths and areas for improvement. The scoring cards may help in the process, and indicate which aspects of **Results** and **Scope** should influence your thinking

Perceived strengths (+)

Perceived areas for improvement (-)

Note: List any relevant measures or comparisons that you feel should be initiated, and are not at present undertaken, as areas for improvement

Results	%
Scope	%
Overall	%

You have now completed Criterion 9 - Note any actions required

Appendix Three: Sources of Further Information

Contact Details

1. **BQC Performance Management Ltd (BQC)**
   P.O. Box 175
   Ipswich
   IP2 8SW
   United Kingdom

   Tel: 00 44 (0) 1473 409962   Fax: 00 44 (0) 1473 833303
   Email: info@bqc-network.com   Web Site: http://www.bqc-network.com

2. **EFQM**
   Brussels Representative Office
   Avenue des Pleiades 15
   1200 Brussels
   Belgium

   Tel: +32 3 775 35 11   Fax: +32 2 779 12 37
   Email: info@efqm.org   Web Site: http://www.efqm.org

3. **BQF**
   32-34 Great Peter Street
   London
   SW1P 2QX

   Tel: +44 (0)171 654 5000   Fax: +44 (0)171 654 5001
   Email: mail@quality-foundation.co.uk   Web Site: http://www.quality-foundation.co.uk

4. **NIST**
   Route 270 and Quince Orchard Road
   Admin Building
   Room A537
   Gaithersburg MD
   20899 USA

   Tel: 0101 301 975 2036   Fax: 0101 301 948 3716
   Web Site: http://www.nist.gov

5. **BESAN (c/o BQC)**
   DuPont Building
   Coldharbour Lane
   Frenchay
   Bristol
   BS16 1QD
   UK

   Tel: +44 (0)117 976 3932   Fax: +44 (0)117 976 3883
   Email: besan@bqc-network.com

Other BQC Publications:

The Excellence Routefinder, Chris Hakes, ISBN 1-902169-05-0

This new publication helps users of the Business Excellence Model focus on what they are trying to achieve and learn from what has worked for others.

Based on many years of sponsored research into the use of the Business Excellence Model coupled with our long track record of facilitating assessments of organisations, it features:-

A collection of best practices and components of success as a series of pragmatic, proven activities that are known to have worked for those who used them
A planning aid and comprehensive tool kit to help the reader define future excellence for his/her own organisation
Simple tools to help prioritise actions and visibly track progress
A unique guide to creating and implementing Visions of Excellence

The Facilitator Support Kit, ISBN 1-902169-05-0

This new publication takes benefit from BQC's extensive experience in facilitating senior management assessment workshops to build a support kit that will help you plan, design and facilitate your own assessment workshops with confidence.

Distilling our vast experience into a'how to' guide it features:
- Lots of practical "do's and don'ts" to help you set up and facilitate a successful workshop
- A step by step guide of what needs to be considered with suggestions on what works best
- A comprehensive set of prompts and searching questions for each of the 32 criterion parts

The Facilitators Complete D.I.Y. Guide.

The Business Driver, ISBN 1-0-2169-02-6

This new publication provides an easy to use Performance Review Programme for small businesses and business units.

32 fact-packed A4 pages lead managers through a Business Performance Review in clear and simple language. It features:
- self-explanatory background presented in a clear and 'graphical' style
- 108 researched and proven questions to enable your manager(s) to gain an insight into what is 'driving' your business
- 40 check questions to validate your manager(s)' assessment from the perspective of employees at all levels

- a unique assessment method that drives actions and improvement without the potentially emotive complication of 'scoring' current performance

"This is an easy and fun way of getting in to Business Excellence"

Charles Higgs, Managing Director, Selected Options Ltd

TQE Data Handling and Analysis Software

The latest version of our assessment software enables new or experienced users of the European Business Excellence Model to display individual and team views of their organisation's performance, leading to consistent and effective data handling and analysis.

It features:
- Simple data entry screens to allow you to capture strengths and areas for improvement
- drag bars and associated text to lead you through the assessment process
- scores that are calculated automatically to benchmark your organisation against the best in Europe
- Hints screens to explain the criteria used in the assessment. Use this as a standard or to tailor the model to suit your experience
- consensus screens that show each person's score for each criterion part plus average score and average total points
- individual assessments that can be combined into a team view using a TEAM processing screen
- Specific team scores which can be used as an individual input to another team to form a hierarchy

CHESTER COLLEGE WARRINGTON LIBRARY

CHESTER COLLEGE WARRINGTON LIBRARY